WRITTEN ARABIC

An approach to the basic structures

WRITTEN ARABIC

An approach
to the basic structures

by

A. F. L. BEESTON

St John's College
University of Oxford

CAMBRIDGE
UNIVERSITY PRESS

Published by the Press Syndicate of the University of Cambridge
The Pitt Building, Trumpington Street, Cambridge CB2 1RP
40 West 20th Street, New York, NY 10011–4211, USA
10 Stamford Road, Oakleigh, Victoria 3166, Australia

Library of Congress catalogue card number: 68–18342

First published 1968
Reprinted 1975 1978 1979 1982 1987 1990 1993

Printed in Great Britain at the
University Press, Cambridge

ISBN 0 521 09559 X

CONTENTS

INTRODUCTION

There already exist a number of manuals of Arabic for English-speaking students, and it might well be thought that an addition to their number was hardly necessary. Teaching experience over some years, however, has suggested to me that there is a large and growing class of would-be students of Arabic for whom none of the existing works is well adapted: namely, those who aspire to a simple reading knowledge of present-day Arabic, as a tool for utilizing recent Arabic writings on their own particular discipline, whether this may be e.g. sociology, history, economics etc. It is not the primary purpose of such students to acquire an ability to write Arabic themselves, nor to read and appreciate a work of purely literary merit; yet at the same time they do need to comprehend what the Arabic writer is saying in as precise a manner as possible.

At the moment, these students are confronted with a choice between two types of Arabic grammar. First, there is the traditionalist type, following the lines of European grammars of Arabic of the nineteenth century, which were themselves modelled on the approach to the language adopted by the Arab grammarians of the eighth century. The latter were, however, not concerned with teaching the basic structures of Arabic to those wholly ignorant of it, but with instilling an understanding of 'correct' usage into those who already knew the language as a mother tongue. The task of acquiring Arabic from a manual of this sort is an extremely burdensome one; the student is required to master an enormous mass of grammatical detail before he can construe even two lines of the sort of text which the class of students I have described above aim at reading, and many abandon the attempt in despair, either through boredom at this painful initial stage, or simply through lack of time to devote to it. By this approach, moreover, the student has forced upon him a mass of knowledge which will in the end turn out to be irrelevant and useless to him for his own particular purposes, however essential it may be for one who aims at becoming an Arabic scholar capable of writing the language and reading the literary monuments of the past.

A second type of available Arabic grammar does indeed concentrate on the modern written language, often by a 'direct' approach, but tends to be slanted exclusively towards newspaper style. Such grammars omit a great deal of information which is required for the precise and scientific comprehension of serious and reflective writing on abstract subjects.

I

In attempting to steer a middle course between these two extremes, I have tried to elicit the basic principles which govern Arabic sentence structure, and to make them intelligible to the English speaker, and to add to this a sufficiency of grammatical detail, at the same time eliminating, or only slightly alluding to, features irrelevant to the main object of the users I have in mind. Nevertheless, I hope it may be possible for those with more extended objectives also to use this work as a first introduction to the language; for it is manifest that the earlier a student gains some basic reading ability, the easier it will be for him afterwards to acquire the finer points. It must be clearly understood that anyone aiming eventually at writing the language and reading the great works of the Arab literary past, will need to supplement this work by the use of other, more conventional manuals.

One result of this economy, and the most revolutionary of them, is the scant attention paid to the variable terminations of words (the so-called *i'rāb*). In existing grammars of all types, this has normally been presented as a fundamental feature of the language, described in the very earliest chapters. It is much to be doubted whether this is in fact the case. Many Arabic speakers are able to comprehend the language as usually written, and yet would have difficulty in giving the text its correct *i'rāb* throughout; evidently therefore their comprehension is achieved without much reliance on the *i'rāb*; and whatever may have been the case in the sixth and seventh centuries, it is probable that since the end of the eighth century this has been a linguistic phenomenon of which the application depends on a previous comprehension of the text and not the other way round. In any case, since a large part of the *i'rāb* phenomena consist of short vowels, which are not shown in the written form of the language as customarily printed, a full and exact knowledge of these phenomena is virtually useless for the student who merely wishes to read ordinary printed material. Moreover, the student who begins by learning to recognize the function of a word in the sentence by means of its *i'rāb*, as is suggested in the available manuals, will find himself encountering an almost insuperable barrier when he tries to make the transition from the fully vowelled specimens of the language in the grammar books to the unvowelled texts of everyday life.

It is for this reason that the policy has been adopted here of employing vowelling as little as possible, in principle only at the first occurrence of a word, or where it is necessary to distinguish between two words with identical consonantal shape when quoted in isolation from a context which would show which one is meant; and no attention is paid to the variable short vowel terminations which occur in nouns, adjectives and imperfect verbs, throughout chapters 1 to 12. At the same time, this policy has not been adhered to with pedantic rigidity, and some short vowels are described even when irrelevant to the main purpose of the book: either because such a description is inextricably linked with the description of features which do appear in the ordinarily written shape of the word (for instance, it is necessary to give an account of the functional principles which govern the use of the forms *abū*, *abī* and *abā*, and it would consequently be of little advantage to omit reference to the fact that similar vocalic variations occur in the short vowels at the end of other nouns); or in certain small details, the omission of which would not appreciably lighten the learner's task (for example, it would be absurd to leave the reader under the impression that the final syllables of *lahum* and *bihim* were pronounced identically, even though he will nowhere see the difference marked in ordinary texts).

Since this work is addressed to mature students, who will wish to pursue their own rhythms of learning rather than to be tied down to a fixed timetable, I have made no attempt to divide the material equally into 'lessons' designed to occupy a stated amount of learning time; the user should spend as much or as little time on each chapter as he needs. Some explanation is called for, however, of the method adopted in the arrangement of the material. The phenomena of Arabic grammar interlock to such an extent that it is virtually impossible to devise a wholly scientific arrangement of watertight compartments; whatever grammatical topic one broaches, one almost always finds that it cannot be fully illustrated without reference to some other topic, and it therefore becomes a matter of arbitrary choice which topic is dealt with first. My overall principle has been to devote chapters to the main phenomena of sentence structure (such as verbs, qualifying clauses, conditionals etc.), and to insert the less significant features wherever seems most convenient, mitigating the effects of this rather arbitrary arrangement by fairly liberal cross-referencing.

No exercise material is included, for two reasons. Firstly, there is the vocabulary problem. Arabic has a fundamental vocabulary of somewhere around a thousand words which will be essential for all users of the language; but above that level one begins to enter into a sphere where the choice of requisite vocabulary is governed by the discipline in which the student is interested: many words which are basic for an economist will be useless for the historian, and vice versa. To insert exercise material adapted to any one discipline would vitiate the usefulness of the book to those concerned with another discipline. Ideally, what is needed is not one body of exercise material, but a set of parallel texts dealing with various subjects. The preparation of such a set, however, is hampered by the present lack of adequate word-counts for Arabic. The only attempt available up to now which is of any use at all is J. M. Landau's *Word count of modern Arabic prose* (New York, 1959), and even this is only useful in eliciting the very commonest words in Arabic, and cannot be used for the construction of a specialist vocabulary of any kind. Computer techniques are required for this purpose, and although several experts are engaged on the study of the application of these to Arabic, the problems involved are still far from solved.

A second reason is that it is highly desirable that the student should at the earliest possible moment move on to work on the actual texts which he desires to read. While therefore a certain amount of 'illustrative' material additional to what is actually included here would no doubt be desirable, if the vocabulary difficulty mentioned above could be overcome, this should only be used to ensure *comprehension* of the principles enunciated in the book*; the actual *training* in the application of those principles is preferably done by analysis of a chosen original Arabic work on the selected discipline, with constant reference back to this book, and with constant practice in the use of a dictionary. It needs hardly to be said that the latter practice should begin at the earliest possible moment; the sole dictionary of any use in this connection is Wehr's *Dictionary of Modern Written Arabic*, in the English version by J. M. Cowan.

Naturally, no description of a language can avoid the use of a grammatical terminology. This is always a difficult problem, and particularly so when one is dealing with a non-European language, for which the conventional European terminology is usually quite unsuitable. So far as Arabic is concerned, almost all its linguistic phenomena fall into categories which do not correspond happily to European grammatical categories, and the use of conventional European terminology is consequently liable to mislead. There is indeed a set of Arabic grammatical terms which have been evolved by the Arab grammarians for the exact description of their language; but one hesitates to burden the beginner's memory with a set of strange sounding words which will be useful only in the context of grammatical description, at a time when he is necessarily striving to memorize the basic general vocabulary. With some reluctance, therefore, I have felt obliged to devise a set of terms specially for this book. My aim in this has been purely pragmatic: to keep them to a minimum required by the nature of the book, and to make them as nearly as possible self-explanatory in the sense of being easily remembered once

---

*The booklet of historical phraseology issued concurrently with this work is a preliminary tentative in this direction.

the initial definition has been read. Neither the terms themselves, nor the definitions, are intended to have a wider relevance outside the immediate purposes of the book.

The conventions of Arabic script are so intimately bound up with Arabic grammatical structure that it is not possible to omit from a grammatical sketch some account of the script. At the same time, the learning of a script is a task of a different kind from that of learning linguistic structure. The section here devoted to the script has to be regarded more in the light of preliminary notes, and of a background sketch to which reference can be made in the grammatical part, than as an autonomous learning tool: for since I suppose hardly any European would be prepared to undertake the learning of Arabic script by an exclusively visual approach (such as could be appropriate to the learning of Chinese ideograms), this part of the learner's task inevitably involves either contact with a native speaker or the use of tape recordings.*

*A Harvard research team has recently investigated the application of methods of 'programmed' learning to Arabic script (J. B. Carroll and G. Leonard, *The effectiveness of programmed 'Grafdrils' in teaching the Arabic writing system*, Laboratory for research in instruction, Graduate School of Education, Harvard, 1963). The report explicitly describes itself as a 'tentative' final version; but the only criticism of it that suggests itself is that the order of the presentation of the Arabic letters is not correlated with the similarities in their written shapes; and any student who can obtain access to this programme together with its accompanying tape recordings would probably find it most helpful.

SENTENCE. A word or group of words constituting a complete and satisfactory communication.

PHRASE. A group of words having its own internal structure and autonomy but not constituting a sentence.

CLAUSE. A word or group of words which in itself would be capable of being a sentence, but is used in a context where it functions only as one element in a larger sentence.

ENTITY TERM. A word or phrase which presents an object of thought to the hearer but without making any statement about it: 'John', 'John's house' and 'the revolutionary policies which the present government is bent on pursuing' are all entity-terms.

PREDICATE. A statement made about an entity-term.

THEME. An entity-term about which a predicate is stated.

NOUN. One type of entity-term consisting of a single word which overtly describes what is intended, such as 'table' or 'centralization'.

NOUN OF SINGLE APPLICATION. A noun which, as between speaker and hearer, is assumed to be applicable only to one precisely identifiable individual entity, such as 'John', 'London'.

NOUN OF MULTIPLE APPLICATION. A noun which in itself is applicable to a variety of individuals within a category of similarly named entities, such as 'house', 'departure'; the hearer's ability to appreciate the individual reference of a noun of multiple application may be the result of its contextual placing, or it may be irrelevant to the nature of the communication [§1 : 2].

PRONOUN. A surrogate or 'shorthand' for an entity-term, of such a nature that the overt entity-term to which it refers is assumed to be detectable by the hearer: 'I' will be understood to refer to the speaker, 'you' to the person addressed, while 'he', 'she', 'it' and 'they' assume that the user is capable, if challenged, of pointing to the overt entity-term for which they stand. The same applies to the associated forms 'me', 'my' etc.

DEMONSTRATIVE. An entity-term which is a surrogate for the gesture of pointing, as in 'give me *that*', '*these* laughed and *those* frowned'. However, a demonstrative is normally capable of being explained by an overt entity-term, and its function therefore differs only marginally from that of a pronoun.

QUALIFIER. A word or phrase attached to a noun, with the function of giving a more ample description of the entity envisaged than the noun itself, without qualifier, would have been capable of conveying; it can be another noun, or an adjective, or a qualifying clause, or a prepositional phrase (see below).

ADJECTIVE. A single word which functions either as a qualifier to a noun (English examples are '*black* book', '*rolling* stone'), or as a predicate. It is not, however, possible to give a linguistically adequate definition of the Arabic adjective in purely functional terms; all that can be said is that some qualifiers behave structurally in the manner described in §1 : 13 and are then classed as nouns, while others behave in a different manner, as described in §1 : 11, and are then termed adjectives.

VERB. A single word, being one of a set of distinctive patterns of word formation, and combining within itself the functions of a predicate and a pronoun theme. This set is subdivided into two parallel sub-sets termed PERFECT and IMPERFECT, but these sub-sets are not 'tenses' in the European sense, since their functions are much wider than that of simply conveying distinctions of time (as is the case with the English differentiation between 'he works' and 'he worked'); see §3 : 19.

VERBAL ABSTRACT. A special type of noun which expresses the underlying concept of a verb, abstracted from all the ideas of time, theme etc. which are implicit in the verb; as in English the verbal abstract in '*love* knows no frontiers' contrasts with the verb in 'we *love* Mary'.

PARTICIPLE. A single word, being one of a set of distinctive patterns of word formation, functioning either as a noun or as an adjective, and having a sense which bears a stable relationship to a verb, as described in §8 : 6.

AGENT. The immediate theme of a verb predicate, not necessarily identical with the theme of the whole sentence.

FUNCTIONAL. A word which, being neither an entity-term nor an adjective nor a verb, signifies relationships between the entity-terms and verbs of the sentence.

PREPOSITION. A single functional word placed immediately before an entity-term, together with which it constitutes a PREPOSITIONAL PHRASE, and having the basic function of indicating relationships between the entity-term and a predicate (as in English 'he arrived *in* London', 'he arrived *from* London'). Prepositional phrases can, however, serve as qualifiers of nouns provided that the latter subsume a predicate (as in 'his *arrival from* London'), and in certain other situations dealt with in chapter 15.

OBJECT. An element in the sentence having the same relationship to a verb as a qualifier does to a noun, namely that of giving a more ample description of what is intended than the verb alone could: 'drinks wine', 'drinks water', 'sits on a chair', 'sits on the floor' are predicates with a greater degree of precision than 'drinks', 'sits', in the same way that 'black book', 'John's house' are more precise than the nouns 'book', 'house'. Objects are termed INDIRECT when they consist of a prepositional phrase, i.e. when the relationship between the entity-term and the verb is indicated by a preposition; or DIRECT when they consist of an entity-term alone without the intervention of a preposition. Both these types of object involve the participation of some entity-term extraneous to the agent of the verb.

INTERNAL OBJECT. A word or phrase which amplifies the idea conveyed by the verb, but without involving the participation of any entity extraneous to the agent, other than the verbal abstract of that verb: in 'John smiled a bitter smile', no entity is involved extraneous to 'John' and the fact of his smiling.

VERBAL SENTENCE STRUCTURE. One in which nothing other than a functional precedes the verb.

THEMATIC SENTENCE STRUCTURE. One in which, in principle, the theme of the statement occupies the initial position after any introductory functional; in some cases, however, this position may be occupied by some other element in the sentence (such as a prepositional phrase) provided that this is not a verb.

NOUN CLAUSE. A clause which functions in the sentence in the same way as a verbal abstract: 'that he will depart' functions in the sentence 'I anticipate that he will depart' in the same way as the verbal abstract 'his departure' in the sentence 'I anticipate his departure'.

CONDITIONAL SENTENCE. One consisting of two clauses, which stand to each other in such a relationship that the validity of the proposition stated in the principal clause is conditioned by the validity or otherwise of the conditioning clause. In 'If you do that, I shall despise you', the statement 'I shall despise you' is a conditioned one which will only be effectively valid provided that the proposition stated in the conditioning clause 'you do that' is effectively realized, and failing this, the statement made in the principal clause will *not* be valid.

HYPOTHETICAL SENTENCE. One of the same structural nature as a conditional sentence, differing from it only in that the probability of the effective realization of the two propositions is presented as remoter and more speculative.

ANTI-CONDITIONAL CLAUSE. One embodying a proposition of which the effective realization does *not* condition the validity of the principal proposition, as in 'even if you do this, I shall despise you', which implies that the statement 'I shall despise you' is a valid one irrespective of whether the proposition 'you do this' is realized or not.

THE ARABIC SCRIPT

§S : 1. Arabic is written from right to left.

§S : 2. The alphabet consists (apart from its first letter, *alif*, on which see below) of letters which are all consonants; but two of them, *w* and *y*, serve a double purpose, being sometimes consonants and sometimes used to denote long vowels *ū* and *ī*.

§S : 3. Short vowels, if indicated at all, are indicated by marks placed above or below the consonant which precedes them in pronunciation. There is a further mark for a 'zero vowel', that is to say, to indicate the situation where the consonant is not followed by any vowel*. In ordinary usage, these marks are rarely written, and the reader is left to guess from such 'unvocalized' script what the actual pronunciation of the word is.

§S : 4. The script is a cursive one, in which normally the letters of a single word are linked together by 'ligatures' as in English handwriting. For this purpose, the functionals *li*, *bi*, *ka*, *wa*, *fa* and *la* are treated as if they were part of the following word; so too is the 'article' [§1 : 1].

§S : 5. There are nevertheless six letters [§S : 11] which are not ligatured to the following letter in the word; consequently a word made up wholly of these letters will appear (as in the case of the printed form of European languages) with each letter written separately.

§S : 6. The alphabet contains a number of pairs and groups of letters which, although they originally had distinctive forms, have come in the evolution of the script to have identical linear shapes. These are distinguished by dots above or below the basic linear form of the letter. Such dots are an integral part of the letter.

§S : 7. A doubled letter is not written twice: doubled pronunciation of a consonant is marked by a special sign placed over it. Many typographers, however, will omit the doubling mark just as one normally omits the short-vowel signs.

§S : 8. The Arabic phonetic system includes a sound (the glottal stop, German 'Vokalanstoss') called *hamz*, which is from the point of view of the structure of the language a fully functioning consonant; and it was this sound that the letter *alif* (the first letter of the Arabic alphabet) originally denoted. But for historical reasons, *alif* has ceased to have that

---

*The exigencies of typography have, however, led in recent years to a tendency towards placing these marks slightly to the left of the position immediately above or below the consonant.

function, and come instead to be the notation for the long vowel *ā*. The consonantal sound *hamz* is consequently denoted by a mark called *hamza* placed, like a short-vowel mark, above or below the line of script.

§S : 9. 'Transliteration' is the practice of using Latin script instead of Arabic script for rendering the language. Apart from its obvious use in European works about the Arabic world, for giving the reader who knows no Arabic some idea of the sound intended, it can be used as a mere typographical expedient to avoid the difficulty and expense of Arabic printing, in works addressed to readers familiar with Arabic and capable themselves of reconstituting the Arabic script form. Since many Arabic sounds are wholly unlike those of English or other European languages, a transliteration addressed to readers who know no Arabic can only be a very vague approximation phonetically; but for the second purpose described above it is possible to use an exact transliteration which aims primarily at indicating the Arabic script form and not the sound, and this is what is employed in most manuals of Arabic grammar. In order to learn the actual sounds intended, one must have recourse to a speaker (or tape-recording), or to a descriptive work such as W. H. T. Gairdner's *Phonetics of Arabic.* Unfortunately, there are a number of different systems of transliteration current, and an Arabic word may appear in a great variety of differing forms in various European language works. For the present purpose, a system is adopted which has some measure of general acceptance in English works about Arabic. The second to twenty-eighth letters of the Arabic alphabet have, in this transliteration, the following conventional order: b t th j ḥ kh d dh r z s sh ṣ ḍ ṭ ẓ ʿ gh f q k l m n h w y. When necessary, the *hamza* is transliterated as '.

§S : 10. Printed Arabic is based (with a few modifications for typographical convenience) on a manuscript style known as *naskh*, which is the Arabic equivalent of 'copperplate'. Everyday handwriting is in a different style, called *ruqʿa*, of which a full analysis is given in T. F. Mitchell's *Writing Arabic* (London, 1953, reprinted 1958). But a learner is best advised to begin by familiarizing himself with the *naskh* and printed style.

§S : 11. The six letters which are not joined to a succeeding letter [§S : 5] are *alif, d, dh, r, z, w.* The forms of these, of the short vowel and the zero-vowel marks, and of the doubling mark [§S : 7], are shown in the Script Tables 1–3.

§S : 12. While the vowel mark for *i* is properly placed below the consonant, many typographers will, for typographical convenience, place it immediately below the doubling mark when the preceding consonant is doubled (Table 3).

§S : 13. The basic letter forms of the other twenty-two consonants may be regarded as those which occur at the beginning of a word, or after one of the six letters mentioned in §S : 11; the combination *l + alif* has however a special shape (Table 4). In traditional script, initial *b*, *t*, *th*, *n*, *y* frequently have their 'hook' inverted when they precede *ḥ*, *j*, *kh* or *m* (Table 9); but this feature is not imitated on the Arabic type-writer, nor in some printed founts.

§S : 14. When one of these twenty-two letters is joined both to the preceding letter and to the following one, the following points should be noted:

(*a*) the ligature is in most cases attached to the base of the succeeding letter (Table 5);

(*b*) however, the ligature from a preceding letter to *r* and *ẓ* joins the tops of these two letters, contrasting with *d* and *dh* which rise after the ligature (Tables 4, 5);

(*c*) in the traditional style, the ligature from a previous letter should be brought over the top of *ḥ*, *j*, *kh* and *m*, so as to join their top left-hand extremity; and many Arabic founts imitate this (Table 6). But other founts, and the Arabic typewriter, use the initial forms of these letters ligatured at their right-hand angle to the preceding letter (Table 7);

(*d*) ', *gh* and *h* in this position have forms differing from those used initially (Table 8).

§S : 15. At the end of a word, twenty of these twenty-two letters (the exceptions being *ṭ* and *ẓ*) take on special forms, mostly characterized by a 'tail' of various shapes (Table 10). Note particularly that the final form of *k* has a mark inside it which resembles the *hamza* mark (S : 8 and Table 11), but must not be confused with it. Final *y*, being unlike any other letter, can and usually does dispense with its characteristic dots (Table 11).

§S : 16. When one of these twenty letters occurs at the end of a word and is preceded by one of the six unligatured letters, their forms are (except for *h*) combinations of the initial form with the final 'tail', as shown in Table 12.

§S : 17. A final *h* with two dots placed over it (and always preceded by the vowel *a*) indicates a pronunciation which fluctuates between *-at* and *-a* [§§1 : 8, 14].

§S : 18. The *hamza* sign is in certain cases written above the central line of script with nothing *on* the line of script vertically level with it; but more often it is 'supported' by a consonantal symbol on the line of script. This symbol may be *alif*, *w*, or a *y* written without its dots. The choice between these possibilities depends on complex rules associated with the vocalic pattern of the word; and there is a good deal of fluctuation of usage in this matter. However, at the beginning of the word, the *hamza* sign is always supported by *alif*, and is placed above the *alif* when the following vowel is *a* or *u*, below it when the following vowel is *i*. The vowel mark is written further away from the line of script than the *hamza* (Table 13).

§S : 19. There is some reluctance to write two *alifs* side by side. Consequently at the beginning of a word the sequence *hamz* + *ā* is denoted by a single vertical *alif*, and a second one placed horizontally above it. Equally, the sequence *hamz* + *a* + *hamz* + consonant is converted into the sequence *hamz* + *ā* + consonant written in the same way (Table 14).

§S : 20. In the middle of a word, the sequence *a* + *hamz* + *ā* is also customarily written with a horizontal *alif* over the vertical one, the *hamza* being then dispensed with (Table 15).

§S : 21. With the sequence *ā* + *hamz* + *a* in the middle of a word, or *ā* + *hamz* + any vowel at the end of a word, it is customary nowadays to write *alif* followed by a *hamza* without support; but some nineteenth-century typographers used the horizontal *alif* in these cases (Table 16).

§S : 22. Arabic does not tolerate a word beginning with a vowel pure and simple; every word begins with either *hamz* or another consonant (the same phenomenon can be heard in the rigorous pronunciation of standard German, 'Bühnendeutsch'). Equally, it has a reluctance to admit an unvowelled consonant as an initial sound (i.e. an initial consonant cluster). In a limited number of cases, therefore, where the first consonant of the word is in principle unvowelled, it is necessary, in order to make the word pronounceable in isolation, to prefix a vowel to it, and this in turn entails prefixing *hamz* to that vowel*. A word like *thnāni* 'two' is regarded by the Arabs as unpronounceable at the beginning of an utterance, and it must take on an initial vowel and *hamz*, becoming 'ithnāni.

§S : 23. When such forms are preceded by another word in the sentence, they no longer need the helping vowel and its *hamz*: for if the preceding word ends in a vowel, the unvowelled initial of the following word forms a syllable with the preceding final vowel, and the syllabification of the juncture *qāla* + *thnāni* is *qā-lath-nā-ni*; if the preceding word would normally end in zero vowel, a vowel is conventionally inserted. But the spelling of such words continues to reflect the pronunciation of it in isolation, inasmuch as the initial *alif* which supports the *hamza* is retained; at the same time, the actual pronunciation is indicated, in full vocalization, by the substitution of a 'juncture' mark (*waṣla*) for the

*In consequence of this, *hamza* at the beginning of a word is often omitted from the transliteration, because an initial vowel in the transliteration *must* imply a preceding *hamz*.

hamza and its vowel, thus showing that these two phenomena are not in fact present even though the *alif* has been retained (Table 17)*.

§S : 24. There are a number of words ending in -*ā*, in which the length of the *ā* vowel is denoted not by *alif* but by *y* (Table 18). This occurs *only* at the end of the word, and should the word receive any additional terminal element, the spelling of the *ā* reverts to the normal one with *alif*.

§S : 25. In some very frequently occurring words, the notation of length of *ā* is omitted altogether by convention (though if it is desired to show this explicitly in full vowel marking, it can be done by writing a small vertical *alif* in place of the short *a* mark). This spelling is invariably used in the word Allāh (see also §1 : 7); almost always in demonstratives [§§2 : 1, 18 : 6]; and frequently in the numeral 'three', *thalāth-* and its associated forms, and in some names such as Sulaymān, Isḥāq etc. (Table 19).

§S : 26. Doubling of the vowel mark at the end of a word is used for the notation of a terminal -*n* following the vowel and having a special grammatical function [§13 : 11]; an *alif* which follows a mark of this kind does not denote vowel length, but is a purely conventional spelling (Table 20). In the case of the *u* mark, it is traditional for the two symbols to be placed inversely in relation to each other (Table 20, first example); but some typographers replace this doubled mark by a symbol illustrated in §13 : 11 in the example 'a man came'. Another instance in which *alif* is purely conventional and does not represent a phonetic reality is mentioned in §3 : 15.

§S : 27. There are a certain number of anomalous spellings, of which the following are the most likely to be encountered:

(i) *mi'a(t)* 'hundred' is normally spelt with an unpronounced *alif* after the *m*; though this convention is often disregarded when it is preceded by a unit numeral, as in 'six hundred' [§18 : 15].

(ii) the word *'idhan* 'then/in that case' can be spelt either with the consonant *n* or with the doubled *a* mark followed by *alif* as described in §S : 26 (Table 20).

(iii) the word for 'son' basically begins with an unvowelled consonant and behaves according to the principles stated in §§S : 22, 23, having normally an initial *alif*. But when it occurs between two names in the formula 'so-and-so son of so-and-so', the *alif* is conventionally omitted (Table 21).

§S : 28. Arabic numerals are written with the highest digit on the left and the unit digit on the right (Table 22).

---

*In the chapters which follow, an initial *alif* without the *hamza* mark is of this nature.

§S : 29. Punctuation has never been standardized in Arabic, and many books still follow the practice of medieval manuscripts in having no punctuation at all apart from the paragraph division. When punctuation is used, it is often used in so unsystematic a manner as to be little help as a guide to sentence structure. Both round brackets and quote marks will sometimes be encountered having not their normal European function of marking parentheses and quotations, but as a device to overcome the absence of capital letters in Arabic script, particularly with European words and names. A question mark is sometimes used in contexts where European usage demands the exclamation.

Script Tables

In the following script tables, the first line of Arabic script is in traditional *naskh* style, with the vocalization and other marks which indicate fully the pronunciation; the second line is in normal print style, without the vowel markings, as will be encountered in ordinary book printing.

ذْ	ذُ	ذِ	ذَ	دْ	دُ	دِ	دَ	(1)
ذ	ذ	ذ	ذ	د	د	د	د	
dh	dhu	dhi	dha	d	du	di	da	
زْ	زُ	زِ	زَ	رْ	رُ	رِ	رَ	
ز	ز	ز	ز	ر	ر	ر	ر	
z	zu	zi	za	r	ru	ri	ra	
	وْ	وُ	وِ	وَ				
	و	و	و	و				
	w	wu	wi	wa				

(2) دارُ دارٍ دارَ رادَ رُودَ

رود   راد   دار   دار   دار

rūda   rāda   dāra   dāri   dāru

وادٍ ذُدْ زُرْ وَدَّ رُدَّ

ردّ   ودّ   زر   ذد   واد

rudda   wadda   zur   dhud   wādi

زَرُّ وَرَدَ وِرْدُ دَوَّرَ

دوّر   ورد   ورد   زرّ

dawwara   wirdu   warada   zarru

(3) وَرِّ/وَرّ ذُرِّ/ذَرّ دَوِرْ/دَوِّرْ

دوّر   ذرّ   ورّ

dawwir   dhurri   warri

(4) با تا ثا نا يا حا جا خا

خا   جا   حا   يا   نا   ثا   تا   با

: khā   jā   ḥā   : yā   nā   thā   tā   bā

سا شا صا ضا طا ظا عا

عا   ظا   طا   ضا   صا   شا   سا

ʿā   : ẓā   ṭā   : ḍā   ṣā   shā   sā

ها ما لَوْ لا كا قا فا غا

ها ما لو لا كا قا فا غا

: hā : mā law lā : kā : qā fā : ghā

يُورَدُ يَرا نَرا ثُرا تُرا بَدا بِلا

يورد يرا نرا ثرا ترا بدا بلا

yūradu yarā narā tharā turā badā bilā

صُورَ شاوَرَ سِرْ خُذْ جَرَّ حُزِّ

صور شاور سر خذ جرّ حزّ

ṣūra shāwara sir khudh jarra ḥuzzi

غُورُ عاوَدَ ظافِرُ طَرَدَ ضِدَّ

غور عاود ظافر طرد ضدّ

ghūru ʿāwada ẓāfiru ṭarada ḍidda

فاها ذِكْرُ كافِرِ قادِرُ فاخِرُ

فاها ذكر كافر قادر فاخر

fāhā dhikru kāfiri qādiru fākhiru

ظاهِرَ

ظاهر

ẓāhira

(٥) كَبِدُ سَبْطُ بَثُّوها لَنا مِيا مَدا

كبد سبط بثّوها لنا ميا مدا

kabidu sabṭu baththūhā lanā miyā madā

كَسا كَذا لَصَوْ عَضُدُ قَطا

كسا كذا لصو عضد قطا

kasā kadhā laṣaw ʿaḍudu qaṭā

قَضا نَفَذَ نَقَدَ بِكَذا نَكا بَلَدُ

قضا نفذ نقد بكذا نكا بلد

qaḍā nafadha naqada bikadhā nakā baladu

(6)
(7) شَجَرُ مَحا فَخِذُ صَمَدُ كَما

شجر محا فخذ صمد كما

shajaru maḥā fakhidhu ṣamadu kamā

(8) سَعْدُ لَغْوُ لَها سَها

سعد لغو لها سها

saʿdu laghwu lahā sahā

(9) بَحْرُ نَجِدُ تَجِدُ يَجُرُّ بِما

بحر نجد تجد يجرّ بما

baḥru najidu tajidu yajurru bimā

(١٠) لِبُّ سَبَّ قُلْتُ بَلَتْ نَفَثَ

لبّ   سبّ   قلت   بلت   نفث

libbu   sabba   qultu   balat   nafatha

بَحْثُ مِنْ لَنْ قُلْنَ جَلَسَ نَفَسَ

بحث   لن   من   قلن   جلس   نفس

baḥthu   lan   min   qulna   jalasa   nafasa

نَبَشَ حَشَّ خَلَّصَ بَعْضُ قَطُّ

نبش   حشّ   خلّص   بعض   قطّ

nabasha   ḥashsha   khallaṣa   ba‘ḍu   qaṭṭu

حَفِظَ خَلْفَ وَصَفَ رَشَقَ حَقُّ

حفظ   خلف   وصف   رشق   حقّ

ḥafiẓa   khalfa   waṣafa   rashaqa   ḥaqqu

بَلْ مَلَّ لَمْ كَمْ شَمَّ تَمَّ

بل   ملّ   لم   كم   شمّ   تمّ

bal   malla   lam   kam   shamma   tamma

ثُمَّ وَجْهُ قَتَلَهُ

ثمّ   وجه   قتله

thumma   wajhu   qatalahu

(۱۱) فَكَّ   بِكَ   شَكَّ   فِي   مَجِى   لِى

فكّ   بك   شكّ   فى   مجى   لى

fakka   bika   shakka   fī   majī   lī

شَى   كَى   سَلْهُ

شى   كى   سله

shay   kay   salhu

(۱۲) مَتَاعُ   فَرَاغُ   بَلَاغُ   مَنَاخُ   تَاجُ

متاع   فراغ   بلاغ   مناخ   تاج

matā'u   farāghu   balāghu   manākhu   tāju

شَرْحُ   شَدَّتْ   قُرْبُ   حَدَثَ   رُوسُ

شرح   شدّت   قرب   حدث   روس

sharḥu   shaddat   qurbu   ḥadatha   rūsu

خَرْشُ   قَصَّ   فَاضَ   حَذْفُ   وَرْقُ

خرش   قصّ   فاض   حذف   ورق

kharshu   qaṣṣa   fāḍa   ḥadhfu   warqu

حَالُ   سَامَ   رَانَ   مِياهُ

حال   سام   ران   مياه

ḥālu   sāma   rāna   miyāhu

(13)

رؤوس	رأس	سئل	سؤال	سأل
ru'ūsu	ra'su	su'ila	su'ālu	sa'ala

أكل	بأس	بئس	بؤس	بئر
'akala	ba'su	bi'sa	bu'su	bi'ru

إيضاح	إنّ	أنّ	إصلاح	أسبوع
'īḍāḥu	'inna	'anna	'iṣlāḥu	'usbū'u

جزء	أوتي
juz'u	'ūtiya

(14)

آمال	آثر
'āmālu	'āthiru

(15)

مآب	رآه
ma'ābu	ra'āhu

(16) سَاءَلَ (سآءل) بَيْضَاءُ (بيضآء)

بيضاء
bayḍā'u

ساءل
sā'ala

قِرَاءَاتُ

قراءات
qirā'ātu

(17) مِنَ ٱلْبَابِ جَلَّ ٱسْمُهُ فَٱجْلِسْ

فاجلس
fa-jlis

جلّ اسمه
jalla-smuhu

من الباب
mina-lbābi

وَٱكْتُبْ

واكتب
wa-ktub

(18) إِلَى عَلَى يَبْقَى الْمَعْنَى الْفَتَى

الفتى
'alfatā

المعنى
'alma'nā

يبقى
yabqā

على
'alā

إلى
'ilā

(19) اللَّهُ هَذَا هَؤُلَاءِ هُهُنَا ثَلَثُونَ

ثلثون
thalāthūna

ههنا
hāhunā

هؤلاء
hā'ulā'i

هذا
hādhā

الله
Allāhu

سُلَيْمٰنُ إِسْحٰقُ

إسحق   سليمن

Isḥāqu   Sulaymānu

(20) وَلَدٌ وَلَدٍ وَلَدًا بِنَاءً إِذًا/إِذَنْ

إذا/إذن   بناء   ولدا   ولد   ولد

'idhan   binā'an   waladan   waladin   waladun

(21) مُحَمَّدُ بْنُ سُلَيْمٰن

سليمن   بن   محمد

(22) ١ ٢ ٣ ٤ ٥ ٦ ٧ ٨ ٩

9   8   7   6   5   4   3   2   1

١٠ ٢,٠٦٤

2,064   10

1

NOUNS AND ADJECTIVES

§1 : 1. An Arabic noun of multiple application can have placed before
it an element *'al*, conventionally termed the 'article', and a noun with
the article is said to be 'defined'. The article has two quite distinct functions, and only the context will indicate which is the appropriate one in
any given case:

(*a*) it may indicate that the individual entity intended is known to
the hearer, either by reason of having been previously mentioned, or by
the factors of the situation in which the statement is made. In this case it
corresponds to English 'the'.

(*b*) it may indicate that the noun is to be taken as applying to any
and every individual of the category named or to the category as a whole.
In this case, English usage fluctuates between 'a', 'the' and absence of
both, as in '*a king* bears heavy responsibilities', '*the elephant* never forgets',
'*man* is mortal'. In all these cases, Arabic uses the article, and in order to
achieve an idiomatic translation it is essential to recognize this use of the
article where it occurs and select the appropriate English form, by possibly
rendering the article as 'a' or omitting it altogether.

§1 : 2. An undefined noun of multiple application does not have the
article in front of it, and implies some unspecified individual or individuals
of the category named, the identity of which is not previously known to
the hearer, as in 'John caught *a fish*', '*a lorry* crashed into the side of the
house', '*some drunks* rolled by'.

§1 : 3. In some contexts, the undefined noun emphasizes the distinction
between singular and plural, as in مَلِك 'one king'; مُلُوك 'several
kings'; يَوْم 'one day'; أَيَّام 'several days'.

§1 : 4. When a noun begins with one of the consonants pronounced
with the tip of the tongue, the *l* of the article changes in pronunciation to
that consonant; the initial consonant of the noun can then be written with
the mark of doubling, yet at the same time the *l* continues to be written
though not pronounced: أَلْنَّاس pronounced '*annās* '(the) men'.

24

§1 : 5. The vowel *a* of the article is present merely to avoid the occurrence of an initial consonant cluster [§S : 22]; when another word precedes it, the vowel is not required and both it and the *hamẓ* cease to be pronounced, nevertheless the *alif* remains in conventional spelling [§S : 23]. An exception to this general rule is the case where the preposition *li* [§S : 4] precedes the article, in which case the *alif* of the article is omitted in spelling. There is therefore a contrast between بالنَّاس *bi-nnās* 'by the men' and لِلنَّاس *li-nnās* 'for the men'.

§1 : 6. Nouns beginning with *l*, when preceded by both the article and the preposition *li*, are written both without the *alif* and also without the *l* of the article. Consequently, only the doubling mark, if used, will distinguish between لِلِسان *li-lisān* 'for a tongue' and لِلِّسان *li-llisān* 'for the tongue'.

§1 : 7. Some nouns of single application have by convention the article in front of them, such as العِراق 'Iraq', but this is a matter of stereotyped expression, and all nouns of single application are by their nature defined, irrespective of whether or not they conventionally have the article. The initial syllable of *Allah* is the article, and is subject to the spelling rules stated in §§1 : 4, 6: hence الله 'God' but لله *lillāh* [§S : 25] 'for God'.

§1 : 8. A large number of nouns have an ending *-a(t)*, of which the *t* is only pronounced in certain circumstances [§1 : 14], being otherwise not pronounced [§S : 17], as in دَوْلَة *dawla(t)* 'realm'. But if a termination is added to such a word, the *t* is pronounced and is then spelt with a normal *t*, as in دَوْلَتِي *dawlatī* 'my realm' [§2 : 16].

§1 : 9. Arabic nouns are grammatically either masculine or feminine. A majority of feminine nouns have the *-a(t)* ending; nevertheless, the differentiation between masculine and feminine is neither exclusively one of meaning nor exclusively one of form. All nouns denoting male persons are masculine, although a few of them have the *-a(t)* ending, such as خَلِيفة 'caliph'. All nouns denoting female persons are feminine, including some which do not have the -a(t) ending, such as أُمّ 'mother'.

Further, there are a few nouns denoting things and not persons, which are grammatically feminine although devoid of the -a(t) ending, the commonest being حَرْب 'war'; دار 'house'; يَد 'hand'; أَرْض 'earth'; نَفْس 'soul/self'; and a few which may be treated either as masculine or feminine, such as حال 'state/condition'.

§1 : 10. When a noun by itself is inadequate to describe the entity term intended, one or more qualifiers may be added. A qualifier can be any one of four things: an adjective, another entity term (noun, pronoun or demonstrative), a qualifying clause, or a prepositional phrase. Except in the case of the qualifying prepositional phrase, the qualified noun invariably precedes its qualifier or qualifiers.

§1 : 11. The adjective adapts itself to the noun which it qualifies in two ways. It takes the -a(t) ending when the qualified noun is grammatically feminine: hence, يَوْم طَوِيْل 'a long day'; تَأْثِير شَدِيد 'a violent effect'; ساعة طويلة 'a long hour'; حرب شديدة 'a violent war'. Secondly, the qualifying adjective must itself have the article when it qualifies a noun which is defined in any way: اليوم الطويل 'the long day'; الحرب الشديدة 'the violent war'; روما القَدِيمة 'ancient Rome' (this noun being grammatically feminine, and also defined by its nature, see §1 : 7).

§1 : 12. A noun followed by another entity term which serves as qualifier to it is said to be 'annexed' to the qualifying term; and the status of annexed noun has important grammatical consequences. In a phrase of this nature, the qualifying noun corresponds to the English forms with apostrophe 's or with prefixed 'of', as in 'Rome's glory' or 'the glory of Rome'; but such phrases in Arabic are indivisible compounds (resembling for example German compound nouns like Staatsminister 'minister of State') and cannot have anything inserted between them as is possible in

English: 'Rome's ancient glory'. An adjective which qualifies an annexed noun must therefore be placed after the qualifying entity term: مَتَجْد

روما القديم 'Rome's ancient glory'.

§1 : 13. Phrases consisting of annexed noun plus qualifying entity term have their status as defined or undefined marked *only* by the qualifying term, and the annexed noun itself *never* has the article. If the qualifying term is an undefined noun of multiple application, then the phrase as a whole, *and* the annexed noun, is grammatically undefined; if it is a noun of multiple application made defined by the article, or a noun of single application, or a defined entity term of any other kind, then the phrase as a whole, *and* the annexed noun, is defined. Hence بَيْت الوَزِير

'the minister's house/the house of the minister'; بيت وزير 'a minister's house/the house of a minister'. It follows that English expressions of the type '*a* house of *the* minister' cannot be represented in Arabic by the annexion structure but use a preposition [§§15 : 3, 4].

§1 : 14. In an annexed noun ending in ة the *t* remains in pronunciation:

دولة مِصْر *dawlat Miṣr* 'the realm of Egypt'; سِكَّة حَدِيد *sikkat ḥadīd* '(road of iron =) a railway'; سكَّة الحديد *sikkat alḥadīd* 'the railway'.

§1 : 15. It is possible to have a whole string of nouns constituting a single structural unit, in which each successive noun is annexed to the following qualifying phrase, itself consisting of annexed noun plus qualifier. The principle about the mark of definition being carried by the last term only [§1 : 13] applies to the whole phrase: مَعْنَى مَقال

وزير دولة 'the sense of a minister of state's speech' is a grammatically undefined entity term, but معنى مقال وزير الدولة 'the sense of the minister of state's speech' and معنى مقال وزير دولة

مصر 'the sense of the speech of the minister of state of Egypt' are defined entity terms.

§1 : 16.   كُلْ is a noun which, when annexed to an undefined noun, conveys the sense of the English adjective 'each/every'; when annexed to a defined entity term, that of English 'all/whole': كل إنـسان 'every human being'; كل ساعـة 'each hour'; كل ملوك 'all the kings of the earth'; كل الحَـقِـيقة الأرض 'the whole truth'.

§1 : 17.   بَعْـض is a noun of anomalous use. It connotes 'one of/ some of' (its implication being ambiguously either singular or plural), and it is annexed to a formally defined entity term, yet contrary to what has been said above, it retains an undefined sense: بعض وُزَراء 'one minister of state/some ministers of state', بعض ملوك الدولة 'one of the kings of the age/some kings of the age', بعض العَـصْـر 'a certain amount of truth'.

أَحَـد (masculine) and إِحْـدَى (feminine) '(some/any-)one' when used alone apply only to persons (the non-personal counterpart being شَىْء 'something/anything'). When annexed, they present the same anomaly as بعض, having a defined entity-term after them yet retaining the undefined sense: أحد الوزراء 'one of the ministers'; إحدى النِساء 'one of the women'.

§1 : 18. أَىّ (masculine) and أَيّة (feminine) are nouns which, when annexed to an undefined singular noun, may be the equivalent of English 'any . . . (at all)': أَىّ رجل 'any man at all'; أَيّة مَرْأة 'any woman at all'. When annexed to a defined plural, they may connote 'any one of . . .' (though other uses also occur, which will be described later): أَىّ الرِجال 'any one of the men'. Both these usages are specially common after negatives [§9 : 10].

§1 : 19. A qualifying noun can also be placed after an adjective, serving to define and limit the range of applicability of the adjective. A qualifying noun used in this way is always defined in form, but does not thereby make the annexed adjective defined, and if the structure of the sentence requires the adjective to be defined, the article must be added to the adjective in the same way as if the qualifying noun were not present [§1 : 11]. Phrases such as واسِع الذِهْن 'broad of mind'; فارِغ الفَهَم 'devoid of understanding' are undefined. Hence وزِير واسِع الذهن 'a broad minded minister'; المرأة الفارغة الفهم 'the woman devoid of understanding'.

§1 : 20. Derived adjectives are formed from nouns by the addition of the termination -īy to the basic noun: ملك 'king', ملكىّ 'royal'; إنسان 'human-being', إنسانى 'human'; عَقْل 'mind/intelligence', عقلى 'mental/intellectual'. In forming the derived adjective it is usual to omit the noun's -a(t) ending, as in سِياسة 'policy', سِياسى 'political'. There are also some anomalously formed derived adjectives, which will be found recorded in the dictionary, such as فَرَنْسا 'France', فَرَنْساوِىّ 'French'.

§1 : 21. There are, however, no words in Arabic which can be said to function exclusively as adjectives: any adjective can in principle be made to function as a noun. أَسْوَد as an adjective means 'black', but can be used also as a noun meaning 'negro'; فرنساوىَ as an adjective means 'French', but can also be a noun meaning 'Frenchman'; كَبِير as an adjective means 'big', as a noun 'old man'. The sense intended can only be determined by the structure of the sentence, inasmuch as an adjectival use can only be present when the word qualifies a *preceding* noun [§1 : 10], or is employed as a predicate [§2 : 2]. Hence, الاسود الكبير 'the big negro'; الكبير الاسود 'the black old man'; اللُغة الفرنساوية 'the French language'; الفرنساوية الجَمِيلة 'the beautiful Frenchwoman'.

§1 : 22. The feminine form of the derived adjective is very commonly employed as an abstract noun, as in إِنْسانية 'humanity'; عقلية 'mentality'. It can also be used as a noun denoting a community of people: from نَصْرانى 'Christian' one has النصرانية 'Christianity/Christendom/the Christian community'.

§1 : 23. The majority of nouns have a plural of a type called 'broken', in which the plural is an independent word formation and not directly related to the singular by the simple addition of a termination (compare English 'man—men' contrasted with the usual plural formations like 'book—books'). Patterns of broken plurals show a great variety, and the broken plural of a given noun must normally be learned separately from the dictionary. Some examples of broken plurals have already been cited: مَلِك 'king', مُلُوك 'kings'; وَزِير 'minister', وُزَراء 'ministers'; يَوْم 'day', أَيّام 'days'; other examples are كِتاب 'book', كُتُب 'books'; نَتِيجة 'result', نَتائِج 'results'.

§1 : 24. Plurals which do not denote persons are treated grammatically as if they were feminine singulars: كتاب مُهِم 'an important book'; كتب مهمة 'important books'; الأيام القديمة 'the old days'.

§1 : 25. A certain number of adjectives have, however, also broken plural forms, such as كَبِير 'big', plural كِبار . Plurals of this kind can be used with reference to persons and to things, so that one may encounter for example بُيُوت كبار 'large houses' as an alternative to بيوت كبيرة .

§1 : 26. An occasionally used alternative to the noun plus adjective structure is one in which the logically qualifying concept is expressed by a noun annexed to the logically qualified concept. As an alternative therefore to الكُتّاب الكبار 'great writers' one may find كبار الكتاب (literally 'great ones of writers').

DEMONSTRATIVES, PRONOUNS AND THE BASIC THEMATIC SENTENCE

§2 : 1. Arabic demonstratives are entity-terms, defined in their own nature, and capable of standing alone as such:

هٰذا (masculine), هٰذِه (feminine)
'this (person)/this (thing)'

ذٰلِكَ (masculine), تِلْكَ (feminine)
'that (person)/that (thing)'

[§S : 25]. Where English uses demonstratives as adjectives, as in 'this minister', 'that day', Arabic treats the nouns as explanatory additions to the demonstrative entity term: such nouns must be nouns of multiple application carrying the article, and are placed after the demonstrative, as in هذا الوزير 'this minister', تلك المرأة 'that woman', هذه الحرب 'this war', ذلك اليوم 'that day'. The plural demonstratives apply only to persons and are the same for both masculine and feminine: هٰؤُلاءِ 'these persons', *أُولائِك النِساء "those women'.

§2 : 2. It has earlier been noticed [§1 : 11] that a qualifying adjective carries the same mark of definition or indefinition as the noun which it qualifies. This principle is specially important, because if an adjective following a defined noun does *not* have the article, it ceases to be a qualifier and becomes a predicate. Whereas هـذا الكتـاب الجَـدِيد 'this new book' is an entity term phrase, هذا الكتاب جديد is a complete sentence conveying the statement 'this book is new'.

*The plural form 'those' is sometimes spelt without the *w*.

§2 : 3. Similarly, an undefined entity term placed after a defined one is a predicate, and the two together constitute a statement: هذا ملك 'this *is* a king'; ذلك شىء غَرِيب 'that *is* a strange thing'; عَمّ مُحمد وزير دولة 'Muhammad's uncle *is* a minister of state'. It is precisely the transition from defined to undefined status that marks the boundary between the entity-term which is the theme under discussion and the predicate stating what it is.

§2 : 4. If a noun following a demonstrative is defined in any other way than by itself having the article [§2 : 1], e.g. by being a noun of single application and so defined by its own nature [§1 : 7], or by being annexed to a defined entity-term [§1 : 13], then this too is a predicate: هذا محمد 'this *is* Muhammad'; هذا وزير الدولة 'this *is* the minister of state'.

§2 : 5. When a defined noun or noun phrase of the nature just described is required to function as explanatory addition to a demonstrative, the order of the two elements is reversed: محمد هذا 'this Muhammad'; سياسة الوزير هذه 'this policy of the minister'.

§2 : 6. Arabic usage does not permit pronouns to receive qualifiers of any kind. An adjective or an entity term, irrespective of whether defined or undefined, which follows a pronoun, is a predicate. The following are therefore all unambiguously statements:

أنا شَخْص مَسْئُول   'I am a responsible person'

أنا الشخص المسؤول   'I am the responsible person'

أنا مسؤول   'I am responsible'

أنا المسؤول   'I am the one responsible'

هُوَ ملك   'he is a king'

هو الملك   'he is the king'

هِـى بِنْت جميلة   'she is a beautiful girl'

هى السياسة الجديدة   'it is the new policy'

Other pronouns are: نَحْنُ 'we'; أَنْتَ 'you' (single male person);

أَنْتِ 'you' (single female person); أَنْتُمْ 'you' (plural male

persons); أَنْتُنَّ 'you' (plural female persons); هُمْ 'they' (male

persons); هُنَّ 'they' (female persons). 'They' referring to things is,

according to the principle of §1 : 24, هى.

§2 : 7. Statements of the kind just described provide a mechanism for the expression of communications involving a defined predicate. The theme is followed by a statement cast in the form of pronoun plus predicate: سُلَيْمـٰـن هو الملك '(Solomon, he is the king =) Solomon is the king'; المرأة هى المسؤولة '(the woman, she is the responsible one =) the woman is the responsible one'. If the pronoun were omitted, these expressions would be taken to mean 'king Solomon', 'the responsible woman'.

§2 : 8. Nevertheless, the pronoun can be omitted when the context is such that no reasonable ambiguity could arise, as for example أَساس سياسة الوزير تَنْفِيذ رَغْبة الملك 'the basis of the minister's policy is the carrying out of the king's wish'. The pronoun is also sometimes inserted, in order to emphasize the structure of the sentence, even when formally unnecessary.

§2 : 9. Prepositional phrases, consisting of a preposition followed by an entity-term, also frequently function as predicates, and when one encounters a defined entity-term followed by a prepositional phrase, there is a distinct possibility that the former is a theme and the latter a predicate: الوزير فِى البيت 'the minister *is* in the house',

هذا فى مقال الوزير 'this *is* in the minister's speech'.

§2 : 10. Prepositional phrases can indeed, as mentioned above, function as qualifiers to a noun [§1 : 10], but this is largely restricted to cases where the qualified noun is a participle, a verbal abstract, or some other abstract noun having a close association with a verb. All these freely take after them as qualifiers the same prepositional phrases as would be appropriate after the corresponding verb (but it should be remembered that qualifying prepositional phrases, unlike other qualifiers, occasionally precede the qualified noun, §1 : 10 and see §10 : 10). Because the verb 'wish' in Arabic requires the preposition فى after it, one can also, using the verbal abstract, write رغبة الملك فى هذا 'the king's wish for this'.

§2 : 11. It follows therefore that the status of a prepositional phrase will often be ambiguous, and it will not be at first sight clear whether it functions as a qualifier of a preceding entity-term, or as a predicate to it. Only the presence or absence of a *subsequent* predicate will resolve this ambiguity and make it clear which function the prepositional phrase has. If رغبة الملك فى هذا is a complete sentence, then the prepositional phrase must be a predicate, and the meaning is 'the king's wish *is* for this'; but in رغبة الملك فى هذا شديدة the presence of the subsequent predicate شديدة indicates that the prepositional phrase is a qualifier, and the meaning is 'the king's wish for this is extreme'.

§2 : 12. When the theme of a statement is an undefined noun and its predicate is a prepositional phrase, the order of the two elements is reversed, the prepositional phrase coming first in the sentence: فى هذا

فى هذه المِنْطَقة 'there is a difficulty in this', صُعُوبة

مُدُن كبيرة 'there are some large towns in this area'.

§2 : 13. In this respect, the following words are treated like prepositional phrases: هُنا هُنالِكَ هُنالِكَ ثَمَّ 'here', and هناك

ثَمَّت (also spelt ثَمَّة) all meaning 'there'. Hence

ثم جَواب لهذه المَسْأَلة 'there is one difficulty'; صعوبة

'there is an answer to this question' (alongside the alternative structure

لهذه المسألة جواب).

§2 : 14. A sentence structure of this kind, using the preposition *li* (or

occasionally عِنْدَ), is the regular way of expressing in Arabic ideas

involving the English verb 'have': للأَمِير بيت كبير (there is

a large house to the prince =) the prince has a large house'. In the case of
this idiom, the placing of the prepositional phrase first is normal even

when the other member of the sentence is a defined term: للعَرَب

فَضْل الأَقْدَمِيَّة فى هذا 'the Arabs have the virtue of

priority in this'.

§2 : 15. A similar structure is used to express ideas of indebtedness or

obligation; the prepositions used are عَلَى in front of the entity term

referring to someone under an obligation in general, عِنْدَ or عَلَى

for a debtor in financial matters, and *li* for a financial creditor. Hence,

على الوزير البَحْث فى هذا الأَمْر (incumbent on the

minister is looking into this matter =) the minister ought to look into this matter'; للأمير على الوزير دينار 'the minister owes the prince a dinar'.

§2 : 16. Pronouns, being merely substitutes for nouns, can like nouns be used as qualifiers; 'his house' is an allusive substitute for 'the house of so-and-so (some identifiable individual)'. But when so used, they have different forms from those listed above [§2 : 6], and take the form of elements attached to the end of the qualified noun and written as one word with it. The forms are -*ī* 'my', -*nā* 'our', -*ka* 'your' (addressed to a single male), -*ki* 'your' (to a single female), -*kum* 'your' (to several males), -*kunna* 'your' (to several females), -*hu* 'his' (or 'its' if the noun alluded to is non-personal but grammatically masculine), -*hā* 'her' (or 'its' if the noun alluded to is non-personal but grammatically feminine, or 'their' if the noun alluded to is a non-personal plural [§1 : 24]), -*hum* 'their' (male persons), -*hunna* 'their' (female persons). If the qualified noun ends in a long vowel or -*ay*, the pronoun qualifier -*ī* is changed into -*ya*; if it ends in -*i*, -*ī* or -*y*, the forms -*hu* -*hum* -*hunna* become -*hi* -*him* -*hinna*. Thus, بيتـى 'my house'; مَعناىَ 'my meaning' [§S : 24]; مَعانيـهـم 'their meanings'.

§2 : 17. In prepositional phrases where the entity term is a pronoun, the latter has forms which in the main resemble those used as qualifiers of nouns, but they combine with the preposition in certain specialized ways:

(i) the prepositions لَدَى 'with' and إِلَى 'to', عَلَى 'on', change their *ā* to *ay* before pronouns: عَلَيـنا 'on us'; إِلَيـه 'to him'; لَدَيـهم 'with them'.

(ii) *li* becomes *la*: لَكُم 'for you'; لَه 'for him/it'.

(iii) the pronoun form -*ī* has the following forms when combined with the prepositions *li* 'for', *bi* 'with', فِى 'in', مِن 'from', عَن 'away from', على 'on', إلى 'to': مِنِّى فِى بِى لِى 'away from', على 'on', إلى 'to'.

إِلَى ٰ عَلَى ٰ عَنِّى. After all other prepositions (virtually all of which end in -a), the -ī entails the disappearance of the -a: مَعَهُ 'together with him'; مَعِى 'together with me'. Other common prepositions of this kind are فَوْقَ 'before', بَعْدَ 'after', فَوْقَ 'above', تَحْتَ 'below', عِنْدَ 'with', بَيْنَ 'between/among'.

§2 : 18. كل is often annexed to pronouns and placed after an entity-term, as a substitute for its annexion to the entity-term itself [§1 : 16]: hence هذا كلّه = هذا كل 'all this'. The same is the case with جَمِيع and بِأَجْمَع (also meaning 'all'): المَصادِر 'all the sources', الوزراء بأجمعهم 'all the ministers'.

§2 : 19. نَفْس in annexion to an entity-term, or annexed to a pronoun and placed after the entity-term, normally conveys the sense of 'same': فى الوقت نفسه or فى نفس الوَقْت 'at the same time'.

§2 : 20. The basic thematic sentence structure implies in itself no definite time indication, and will be found in various contexts alluding to past, present or future time.

3

THE VERB

§3 : 1. The sentence structures described in chapter 2 consist of two separate and clearly recognizable elements, theme and predicate. The Arabic verb, however, is an amalgam of several meaningful elements combining in one word both a predicate and a pronoun constituting a theme of the predicate, as well as indications of time and modality associated with the predicate and conveyed by a differentiation between two sets of forms, the 'perfect' and 'imperfect'.

§3 : 2. When the theme pronoun implied in the verb alludes to the speaker or person addressed, the theme is fully intelligible, and a single word can thus constitute a full sentence: expressions like 'I smile', 'you smiled' are in Arabic single words which may themselves be full sentences. This is equally the case when the implied theme pronoun alludes to a person or thing (or persons or things) extraneous to the speaker and person addressed, provided that the noun to which the pronoun alludes is clear from the context: the Arabic verbs meaning 'she died', 'it failed' can be full sentences provided that the entity terms alluded to by 'she' and 'it' are clear from the context. If this is not the case, then it is necessary to add an overt entity term to clarify the theme pronoun implied in the verb. This entity term may precede or follow the verb. When it precedes, it functions as a theme and the verb is a predicate-clause in which the implied pronoun alludes back to the overt theme; consequently a sentence like الاميرة ماتَت 'the princess, (she) died' is a structure parallel to the one described in §2 : 7, سليمن هو الملك 'Solomon, (he) is the king'. When the overt entity-term follows the verb, it is a clarificatory addition explaining the allusion of the pronoun implied in the verb: ماتت الاميرة 'she died, (namely) the princess'.

§3 : 3. It must however be appreciated that when a theme has been enunciated and followed by a verbal predicate clause, the pronoun which alludes back to the theme may be found anywhere in the predicate clause, and is not necessarily the pronoun implied in the verb, since the

39

latter may have its own clarificatory entity-term explaining the agent

pronoun implied in the verb: الاميرة ماتت أمّها is 'the mother

of the princess died' (it has to be analysed as 'the princess—she died,
namely, her mother').

§3 : 4. Whereas European languages envisage the verb as a predicate
stating an *event* which involves the agent, many Arabic verb forms are
descriptive in their nature, with an emphasis on what the agent *is* rather
than on what it *does*, and are therefore congruous in sense with an
adjective predicate of the kind mentioned in chapter 2. Hence, for the
communication 'its meaning is clear' one may find the predicate in verbal

form* as يتّضح معناه or معناه يتّضح, as well as معناه

واضح with adjective predicate.

§3 : 5. Every Arabic verb and noun is theoretically derivable from a
'root' consisting of consonants only. In the great majority of cases the
root is three consonants, though there is a handful of nouns having only

two consonants, like يد 'hand', and a certain number of four-consonant

roots. The actual form of any given word is created by filling out the
root consonants with vowels and sometimes additional consonants which
are not part of the root. In order to describe the actually occurring word

formations, it is customary to use the consonants ف . ع . ل as

ciphers typifying the root consonants, and hence to say, for example, that

كِتاب 'book', قِتال 'battle', and جِبال 'mountains' are all

of the 'pattern' فِعال.

§3 : 6. Arabic dictionaries list all nouns and verbs under these

theoretical roots. Consequently, a noun like مَسْألة 'question', which

is of the pattern مَفْعَلة, will be found in the dictionary under the

*See §§3 : 8, 3 : 12 (v) for the explanation of this verb form.

entry س . ء . ل. For the purposes of dictionary arrangement, *hamza*, though not strictly an alphabetic letter, is treated as the first letter of the alphabet, so that the entry س . ء . ل precedes the entry ت . ب . س.

§3 : 7. From the consonantal root can be derived a number of types of verb. These have been conventionally numbered I to X, an arrangement not entirely happy, but one which it is necessary for the learner to follow, because it is used in Wehr's dictionary. Type I consists of the root consonants filled out by a vowel pattern in which the first vowel is *a*, the following consonant is unvowelled in the imperfect, and the quality of the second vowel differs as between one verb and another; hence one has such varieties of pattern as

	Perfect	Imperfect	Verbal abstract
'work'	عَمِلَ	يَعْمَل	عَمَل
'write'	كَتَبَ	يَكْتُب	كِتابة
'ask'	سَأَلَ	يَسْأَل	سُؤال

Dictionaries consequently cite the second vowel of both perfect and imperfect for Type I verbs, commonly by giving in full the form of the perfect which implies the pronoun 'he', and putting after this the vowel which is the second vowel of the imperfect. The verbal abstract entity-term corresponding to a Type I verb is also fluctuating in pattern, and this too is usually given in dictionaries; Wehr places this item of information in brackets after the perfect and the second vowel of the imperfect. Other types of verb are constant in their patterns, so that if one is told that a verb is of Type V from a given root, one can automatically construct its forms and that of its corresponding verbal abstract. Wehr therefore indicates such forms simply by the numbering of the verb-type in bold roman figures, without further detail.

§3 : 8. Verb types other than I have the following patterns for the perfect and imperfect implying the pronoun 'he', and the verbal abstract:

Type	Perfect	Imperfect	Verbal abstract
II	فَعَّلَ	يُفَعِّلِ	تَفْعِيل
III	فاعَلَ	يُفاعِلِ	مُفاعَلة
IV	أفْعَلَ	يُفْعِلِ	إفْعال
V	تَفَعَّلَ	يَتَفَعَّلَ	تَفَعُّل
VI	تَفاعَلَ	يَتَفاعَلَ	تَفاعُل
VII	انْفَعَلَ	يَنْفَعِلِ	انْفِعال
VIII	افْتَعَلَ	يَفْتَعِلِ	افْتِعال
IX	افْعَلَّ	يَفْعَلَّ	افْعِلال
X	اسْتَفْعَلَ	يَسْتَفْعِلِ	اسْتِفْعال

which can be exemplified as shown opposite.

§3 : 9. The meanings of each of the verb types derived from a single root must be learned independently. Analysis of the meanings of the various verb types derived from one root will usually reveal some element of common meaning between them, but the actual sense of each type cannot be deduced and must be ascertained from the dictionary (just as in English, although 'overtake' and 'undertake' have both some relationship to the idea of 'take', the actual sense of these two verbs could not be discovered by a foreigner otherwise than from a dictionary).

§3 : 10. There are certain kinds of root where the application of the normal patterns of word formation is subject to modifications. These are principally (i) roots containing one or more of the 'weak' consonants *w* and *y*, (ii) 'doubled' roots, in which the second and third consonants

Type	Root	Perfect	Imperfect	Verbal abstract
II 'think'	ف.ك.ر	فَكَّرَ	يُفَكِّرُ	تَفْكِير
III 'fight'	ق.ت.ل	قَاتَلَ	يُقَاتِلُ	مُقَاتَلَة
IV 'perceive'	ب.ص.ر	أَبْصَرَ	يُبْصِرُ	إِبْصَار
V 'learn'	ع.ل.م	تَعَلَّمَ	يَتَعَلَّمُ	تَعَلُّم
VI 'become acquainted'	ع.ر.ف	تَعَارَفَ	يَتَعَارَفُ	تَعَارُف
VII 'depart'	ص.ر.ف	اِنْصَرَفَ	يَنْصَرِفُ	اِنْصِرَاف
VIII 'believe'	ع.ق.د	اِعْتَقَدَ	يَعْتَقِدُ	اِعْتِقَاد
IX 'be red'	ح.م.ر	اِحْمَرَّ	يَحْمَرُّ	اِحْمِرَار
X 'use'	ع.م.ل	اِسْتَعْمَلَ	يَسْتَعْمِلُ	اِسْتِعْمَال

are the same letter. Many dictionaries, including Wehr, list doubled roots

as if they were two-consonant ones, so that ر . ر . ق precedes in the

alphabetical arrangement ء . ر . ق and ب . ر . ق.

§3 : 11. The modifications to which such roots are subject in the formation of words can be stated in terms of rules, and the best account of
these rules is to be found in R. Blachère's *Eléments d'arabe classique* in
the chapters devoted to 'Racines anormales'. But the rules are complicated,
and since many of them affect only the vowel pattern of the word, they
are of little help to a reader confronted only with unvocalized text. For
the latter, the main points to be noted are that in some word forms the
consonant *w* or *y* may be merged into a long vowel or eliminated completely from the written shape of the word; and that in the case of doubled
roots, the second and third root consonants sometimes coalesce into a
doubled consonant, which may or may not (at the typographer's whim)
be indicated by the mark of doubling.

In the case of verbal abstracts from roots of this kind, two very
commonly occurring phenomena should be noted: (i) in the verbal
abstract of Type IV and X verbs from roots having *w* or *y* as second
consonant, the second root letter is merged into a long *ā*, and the termina-

tion -*a*(*t*) is added; so that from root د . ى . ف one has the Type IV

verb أَفَادَ 'he benefitted/informed' and the Type X verb اسْتَفَادَ

'he gained/made use of', of which the verbal abstracts are respectively

إفادة and اسْتِفَادة; (ii) the verbal abstracts of Type II verbs

from roots with *w* or *y* as third consonant have the pattern تَفْعِلة

as in root ى . م . س, Type II verb سَمَّى 'he named' [§3 : 27]

verbal abstract تَسْمِية; and there are one or two other roots which

show the same phenomenon, e.g. جَرَّبَ 'he experienced', with verbal

abstract تَجْرِبة.

§3 : 12. In addition to roots of the above mentioned kinds, certain other classes of root entail modifications of the normal word patterns, which can be stated fairly simply:

(i) when the first consonant of the root is one of the four letters ص ض ط ظ, the ت of the Type VIII verb becomes ط so that from root ض . ر . ب one has a Type VIII verb اضْطَرَبَ 'he fell into confusion'; from root ط . ل . ع, Type VIII verb اطَّلَعَ 'he became cognizant'.

(ii) when it is د, the ت of the Type VIII verb becomes د which coalesces with the د of the root to give a doubled letter: from root د . ع . م the Type VIII verb is ادَّعَمَ 'he supported himself'.

(iii) when it is ذ, the ت of the Type VIII verb coalesces with it to produce either doubled د or doubled ذ: from root ذ . ك . ر the Type VIII verb is ادَّكَرَ or اذَّكَرَ 'he remembered'.

(iv) when it is hamza, the latter is merged into a long vowel in the perfect of the Type IV verb and its corresponding verbal abstract: from root ء . ث . ر one has the Type IV verb آثَرَ 'he preferred' and the verbal abstract إيثار 'preference'.

(v) when it is و, this becomes ت throughout the Type VIII verb: root و . ز . ن, Type VIII verbal abstract اتِّزان 'poise'.

§3 : 13. There are hardly any true irregular verbs in Arabic, and the only ones likely to be encountered in ordinary reading are:

(i) root ر . ء . ى, Type I verb رَأَى 'he saw', omits the *hamza* in its imperfect, which is يَرَى (and *not*, as it would be according to the normal pattern, يَرْأَى).

(ii) same root, Type IV verb, omits the *hamza* in both perfect and imperfect: أَرَى 'he showed', imperfect يُرِى.

(iii) root ذ . خ . ء, Type VIII verb, changes the *hamza* to ت, giving اتَّخَذَ 'he took'.

§3 : 14. The implied pronouns in verb forms are indicated by variations in the pattern of the word which in the perfect affect the termination only, but in the imperfect affect either the beginning only or both beginning and termination of the word. These variations are exemplified for the perfect by:

-a	عَلِمَ	'he knew'
-at	طَلَبَتْ	'she sought'
-ta	أَرْسَلْتَ	'you (one male) sent'
-ti	عَرَفْتِ	'you (one female) recognized'
-tu	كَتَبْتُ	'I wrote'
-ū	عَمِلُوا	'they (male persons) worked'
-na	ذَهَبْنَ	'they (female persons) went'
-tum	حَمَلْتُمْ	'you (males) carried'

-tunna	ظَهَرْتُنَّ	'you (females) appeared'
-nā	بَلَغْنا	'we reached'

§3 : 15. The final *alif* which appears at the end of the -*ū* termination is simply a convention of writing and is not pronounced. It is used only at the end of the word, and disappears if any further termination is added to the word. The same convention applies to all verb forms in which -*ū* comes at the end of the word, provided that plurality is implied.

§3 : 16. The variations in the beginning of the imperfect forms are consonants. The vowels which follow these consonants vary according to the verb type, as can be seen from the list in §3 : 8. The imperfects corresponding to the perfect forms listed in §3 : 14 are:

y-	يَعْلَم	'he knows'
t-	تَطْلُب	'she seeks'
t-	تُرْسِل	'you (one male) send'
t- ... -īna	تَعْرِفِين	'you (one female) recognize'
ʾ-	أَكْتُب	'I write'
y- ... -ūna	يَعْمَلُون	'they (males) work'
y- ... -na	يَذْهَبْن	'they (females) go'
t- ... -ūna	تَحْمِلُون	'you (males) carry'
t- ... -na	تَظْهَرْن	'you (females) appear'
n-	نَبْلَغ	'we reach'

§3 : 17. An overt entity-term to which the pronoun implied in the verb alludes can [§3 : 2] precede or follow the verb. If it precedes, then the verb takes on a pronoun form strictly adapted to the nature of the entity-term, and is plural if the entity-term denotes persons, though the principle stated in §1 : 24 continues to apply when it is non-personal. But if the verb precedes the clarificatory entity-term, the verb-form is always singular.

الوزراء أرسلوا or أرسل الوزراء 'the ministers sent'

النساء انصرفن or انصرفت النساء 'the women departed'

النتائج تظهر or تظهر النتائج 'the results appear'

§3 : 18. When the following clarificatory entity-term is grammatically feminine, the preceding verb is commonly feminine singular, but instances may occasionally be encountered in which it has the masculine form, particularly if other words intervene between the two: يظهر من دَرْس هذا الكتاب نتائج مهمّة 'there appear from the study of this book some important results'. On the other hand, the reader may occasionally encounter cases in which a noun denoting a precisely definable group of people has a feminine singular verb: أقامَت التُرْك السَلاجِقة دولة 'the Seljuk Turks established a state'.

It is furthermore normal for كل ٰ and بعض [§§1 : 16, 17], when annexed to feminine entity-terms, to be themselves treated as feminine: انصرفت كلّٰ هؤلاء النساء 'all these women departed', نَشَأَتْٰ بعض الصعوبات 'certain difficulties arose'.

§3 : 19. The sense differentiation between perfect and imperfect operates on three levels, and in various contexts any one of these levels of differentiation may receive the main emphasis, overshadowing or virtually eliminating the others:

(i) the perfect points to past time, the imperfect to present or future time.

(ii) the perfect points to a single action, regarded as instantaneous in its occurrence, the imperfect to habitual or repeated action, or to one visualized as covering a space of time.

(iii) the perfect points to a fact, the imperfect to a conceptual idea not necessarily realized in fact, and will often have to be rendered in English by 'can/might/may/would/should . . .'.

§3 : 20. In older Arabic, the perfect verb was sometimes used to convey an aspiration, but this is hardly ever encountered in modern writing outside a small range of stereotyped expressions, such as الله رَحِمَهُ 'may God have mercy on him' [§3 : 25], used when mentioning a deceased Muslim.

§3 : 21. It can be made explicit that the imperfect is being used with reference to future time by placing *sa-* or سَوْفَ before it, though this is not necessary if the context sufficiently indicates futurity. سنذهب or نذهب سوف means explicitly 'we shall go', whereas نذهب alone is capable of also meaning, according to the requirements of the context, 'we are (now) going', 'we (habitually) go', 'we could go', 'we might go', 'we were going', 'we used to go'.

§3 : 22. The perfect can intrinsically be used either as a narrative form detailing past events ('he died'), or descriptively to picture a situation arising from an anterior event ('he has died', or, in an appropriate context, 'he had died'). If it is used descriptively, this can be made explicit by placing before it قَدْ or لَقَدْ: عَلِمْنَا قد علمنا 'we knew'; 'we have come to know' (descriptive of the present situation resulting from a previous accession of knowledge)*.

§3 : 23. قد placed before an imperfect reinforces the concepts of habituality or potentiality inherent in that form [§3 : 19 (ii, iii)]. In

---

*The differentiation between the 'narrative' and the 'situational' use of the perfect cannot always be conveyed in English. We do distinguish between the narrative 'he died', 'it became clear' and the situational 'he had died', 'it was clear', but when an Arabic author might well write قد مَلَكَ منطقة واسعة since this describes a situation, we would normally write simply 'he controlled a wide area'.

English it may have to be rendered in this case by such terms as 'possibly/ probably/occasionally/often' etc.: قد تفكر 'you may well think/ you will sometimes think' etc.

§3 : 24. Just as the noun may require a qualifying expression to describe fully what is intended [§1 : 10], the verb may require additional expressions in order to explain fully what is meant, in the shape of an object or objects, whether direct, indirect or internal. Arabic usage in this respect is highly idiomatic and careful attention must be paid to it: where an English verb requires a direct object the corresponding Arabic verb may require an indirect object and vice versa; and a verb followed by one preposition will often have a completely different meaning from the same verb used with another preposition or with a direct object. Wehr carefully records these usages. In Wehr, as in many other dictionaries, the letter form ﻩ is used as a conventional symbol for a personal direct object, ﻪ for a non-personal one.

§3 : 25. If the entity-term which functions as direct object of a verb is a pronoun, the latter has the same form as it would have when functioning as qualifier to a noun [§2 : 16], except that the pronoun form -*ī* is in this case replaced by -*nī*: أرسلني 'he sent me'; بلغتنا الأخبار 'the reports reached us'; كتبه الوزير 'the minister wrote it'; عرفتُه 'I recognized him/it'. In the perfect verb form terminating in -*tum* [§3 : 14] this becomes -*tumū*- before an object-pronoun: عرفتموها 'you (male persons) recognized her/it/them (non-personal)'.

§3 : 26. A pronoun implicit in a verb, or an object pronoun or qualifying pronoun, or one attached to a preposition, can be specially emphasized by placing after it the corresponding pronoun form from the set described in §2 : 6: أقول لك أنت 'I tell *you*'; أقول لك أنا '*I* tell you'; أرسلونا نحن 'they sent *us*'; بيتى أنا '*my* house'.

§3 : 27. When a root has *w* or *y* as third consonant, the perfect verb form implying the pronoun 'he/it (masculine)' in all verb types other than

Type I merges the third root consonant into a long vowel -ā spelt with ى if it comes at the end of the word, but with ا when object pronouns are added. The perfect verb form implying the pronoun 'she/it (feminine)' omits the third root letter altogether. From root ن . ق . ى one has therefore the Type VIII verb forms اِنْتَقَى 'he chose', اِنتقاه 'he chose it', اِنتقَتْ 'she chose'. The same is true of Type I verbs from such roots, with two exceptions: (i) when the third root consonant is *w* the masculine form is spelt with ا, so that from root ب . د . و one has بَدَا 'he appeared', بَدَتْ 'she appeared'; (ii) if the variable vowel of the Type I perfect is *i*, the third root consonant is retained as *y*, so from root ر . ض . و one has رَضِىَ 'he was content', رَضِيَتْ 'she was content'.

§3 : 28. It will be noticed that the principles enunciated above will require the reader to distinguish between اِنتقانا 'he chose us' and اِنتقينا 'we chose'.

§3 : 29. One point that will be further elaborated later deserves a summary mention here. This is that direct object status of an undefined noun (and of an adjective which qualifies such a noun) is marked in certain circumstances by the addition of a terminal *alif*. One must distinguish therefore between أرسل إلىَّ رجل 'some man sent (a message) to me' and أرسل إلىَّ رجلا 'he sent a man to me'.

§3 : 30. The relative placing of the agent entity-term and the direct object entity-term (not being a pronoun) after the verb is not governed by any strict rule; and the reader must expect to encounter cases where the direct object term precedes the agent term, as well as vice versa (an example is given in §8 : 18).

4

QUALIFYING CLAUSES AND SIMILAR STRUCTURES

§4 : 1. A qualifying clause has the same function as an adjective, but does so by means of a structure which could in itself stand as a statement, and which in principle contains within itself a pronoun alluding to the qualified noun. When the qualified term is an undefined noun or undefined noun phrase, the simple juxtaposition of the clause to the qualified noun or phrase is sufficient to indicate the qualifying function of the clause. It can be assumed that in the vast majority of cases, if an undefined expression is immediately followed by a sentence structure containing a pronoun which alludes to it, the sentence structure is a qualifying clause to that undefined expression; whereas in the type of sentence in which a clause functions as predicate [§§3 : 2, 3], the theme term is normally defined. Hence الاميرة ماتت أمّها is a full statement, with الاميرة functioning as theme and ماتت أمها as its predicate, and means 'the princess' mother died'; whereas أميرة ماتت أمها is not a full statement, but an entity-term in which أميرة is a qualified noun and ماتت أمها a qualifying clause, and it means 'a princess whose mother died'.

§4 : 2. The pronoun, within a qualifying clause, which alludes to the qualified noun, is not necessarily overt, but may be implicit in a verb form: وزير حَصَلَ على النّجاح 'a minister who has achieved success'.

§4 : 3. When the qualified noun or noun phrase is defined, the qualifying clause has exactly the same structure as in the case of an undefined qualified term, but its status as qualifying clause (and not as predicate) is marked by the insertion in front of the qualifying clause of الّذى (when the qualified term is grammatically masculine), or الّتِى (when the qualified term is a single female person or a grammatically feminine non-personal term or a non-personal plural), or الّذِين (when the qualified term denotes male persons), or اللّاتِى (when the qualified term denotes female persons): الوزراء الذين حصلوا على النجاح 'the ministers who have

52

achieved success'. The following structures should be studied; in the case
of the thematic structures (*b*), (*c*) and (*d*) the boundary between the
theme and the predicate is indicated by the vertical line:

(*a*) حصلنا على هذه النتائج لِمَـنْـفَـعَـة القَـوْم 'we have achieved these
results for the benefit of the nation'.

(*b*) هذه النتـــائج | حصلنا عليها لمنفعة القوم 'these results we have
achieved for the benefit of the nation'.

(*c*) هذه النتائج التى حصلنا عليها | لمنفعة القوم 'these results which we
have achieved are for the benefit of the nation'.

(*d*) هذه | نتائج حصلنا عليها لمنفعة القوم 'these are some results which
we have achieved for the benefit of the nation'.

§4 : 4. The الذى group of forms can also function as entity-terms in
their own right, without a preceding noun; the singular forms التى الذى
may have either a personal or a non-personal implication:

الذى نعتقده 'the thing which we believe'

الذين نعتمد عليهم 'the persons on whom we rely'.

This group of forms is subject to the spelling convention described at the
end of §1 : 5. Hence, للذين نعتمد عليهم 'for the persons on whom we
rely'.

§4 : 5. Modern usage sanctions the use of demonstratives both in front
of a noun qualified by an الذى etc. clause, and in front of the الـذى forms
when used without a qualified noun:

تلك المرأة التى تعرفها 'that woman whom you recognize'

ذلك الذى أخبرتهم به 'that thing of which you informed
them'

§4 : 6. In lieu, however, of the use of the الذى etc. forms as entity-
terms in the manner described in §4 : 4 (but *not* when they are used as in
§4 : 3), one will very commonly find مَـنْ or ما. These two words are
differentiated in a way unlike those: whereas the الذى group distinguishes
between masculine and feminine and between singular and plural, but
does not distinguish in the singular between a personal and a non-
personal allusion, on the other hand مَـن has a personal allusion and ما a
non-personal one, but neither of them distinguishes whether the allusion

is to singular or plural, masculine or feminine. The type of allusion intended can, it is true, be made explicit by the nature of the pronoun within the clause: مَن نعتمد عليهنَّ 'the (female) persons on whom we rely'. Nevertheless, it is extremely common to use a masculine singular pronoun within the clause referring to مَن or ما, irrespective of whether the allusion intended is to singular or plural, masculine or feminine. Consequently, مَن نعتمد عليه is capable of meaning 'the person or persons, male or female, on whom we rely', and ما نعتمد عليه 'the thing or things, masculine or feminine, on which we rely'.

§4 : 7. A further point of differentiation between the الذى forms and ما/مَن is that the former always have defined status, whereas the latter may be either defined or undefined in sense, and may consequently imply either 'the person/thing ... who/which' or 'a person/thing ... who/which'.

§4 : 8. There are two structures in which it is permissive to omit the pronoun within the clause which refers back to the introductory الذى or ما/من : (i) when the pronoun functions within the clause as theme, the predicate of which is a prepositional phrase, as من هو فى البيت or من فى البيت 'the person who is in the house'; (ii) when it functions as direct object of the verb in the clause, as ما نعتقده or ما نعتقد 'the thing(s) which we believe'.

§4 : 9. A specially frequent structure is the avoidance of a defined noun qualified by a clause introduced by الذى etc., and the employment, as an alternative, of a ما/مَن clause followed by the preposition مِنْ plus the plural of the category noun which in the English structure is the qualified term. Instead therefore of الوزراء الذين كتبت اليهم 'the ministers to whom I have written' one will very commonly find مَن كتبت اليه ;مِن الوزراء instead of الأخبار التى بلغتنى أمْسِ 'the reports which reached me yesterday', ما بلغنى أمس مِن الاخبار.

§4 : 10. When the preposition فى precedes ما or من, the two are often written as one word: فيما فيمن. The same is the case with the prepositions

مِن and عن, with the additional feature that the *n* of the preposition becomes *m*, hence عمَّا عمَّن ممَّا ممَّن.

§4 : 11. أَىّ (masculine) and أَيّة (feminine) 'whichever, whatever', with either personal or non-personal reference, can in principle function like ما/مَن, but are most commonly used in annexion to an entity-term, as in حَلَّلَ أية صعوبة وقعت 'he solved whatever difficulty occurred'; نعتمد على أيّهم يَسْتَطيع هذا 'we rely on whichever of them can do this'.

§4 : 12. When الذى or مَن has reference to the speaker or person addressed, Arabic idiom often employs the corresponding pronoun within the clause following (contrary to English practice):

أنت مَن تستطيع هذا 'you are a person who *is* able to do this'

أنا الذى يعرفنى كلّهم 'I am the one whom all of them know'

5

CONNECTIVES

§5 : 1. Connectives link words, phrases or sentences in such a way that each of the connected members has precisely equal syntactic and functional status. The three basic Arabic connectives are و and فَ 'and' [§§5 : 4], and ثُمَّ 'and (subsequently)'. But the range of usage of و and فَ is much wider than that of English 'and'. و will often be found in contexts where English would use a non-emphatic 'but' or 'or'. And whereas و simply links two items without implication as to the priority of one over the other, فَ implies that what precedes it has some sort of priority over what follows it; when the priority intended is one of time, فَ marks the independent stages in a sequence of events, as in قَامَ الوزيرُ عن مَجْلِسه فأنصرف 'the minister rose from his seat, and departed'. The priority can also, however, be one of logical sequence of the train of thought, and this can work in either of two ways: the mind can proceed from a cause to a consideration of its effect, and in this case فَ corresponds to English 'so', as in قد أدْلَيْتَ بحُجّة قاطعة لهذا فأعتقده 'you have adduced a decisive argument for this, so I will believe it'; or alternatively, the mind can proceed from a phenomenon to a consideration of its cause or justificatory generalization, and in this case فَ corresponds to English 'for', as in قد أخْطَأْت فالخَطَأَ إنسانيّ 'you have erred, for to err is human'. This second usage is specially common when the second proposition begins with إنّ [§6 : 3 (i)].

§5 : 2. Furthermore, و and فَ are not invariably connectives in the sense outlined above, for from time to time they serve to mark structural divisions within a sentence, and in such cases they must *not* be translated in English as 'and' etc. One instance of this phenomenon is that if a prepositional phrase is placed first in the sentence (otherwise than in the structure described in §2 : 12–15), it is common to mark the beginning of

'in على كل حال فالجواب واضح :ف the main structure of the sentence by
any case, the answer is obvious'. Other instances will be mentioned later
[§§6 : 3 (iii), 11 : 1, 12 : 1–2, 12 : 14].

§5 : 3. No two of the connectives mentioned above can stand in
immediate juxtaposition with each other. If therefore the reader encounters وثَمّ, the inference is that ثَمّ 'there' is intended [§2 : 13], and
not the connective ثُمّ.

§5 : 4. لٰكِنْ [§§: 25] and ولكن imply a strong 'but' or 'nevertheless':
قد يصحّ هذا ولكن أَشُكّ فيه 'this may possibly be true, nevertheless
I doubt it'.

§5 : 5. بَلْ is a connective implying that the proposition which
follows it is to some degree more exactly correct than the one preceding
it: نكرَه هذا بل نرفُضه بالجُمْلَة 'we dislike this, or rather, we reject it
altogether'.

§5 : 6. أَوْ is a connective linking two items which are mutually exclu-
sive possibilities, of such a nature that they could be marked in English
by 'either . . . or alternatively . . .': قد تصحّ قِصّته أو تزيف 'his story
may be true or false'. Modern usage, however, tends to extend the use of
أو to all contexts where English uses 'or'. And just as in English 'or' can
be reinforced by a preceding 'either', this can be represented in Arabic by
إمّا فى مصر أو فى الشَّأم :إمّا 'either in Egypt or in Syria'. When this
introductory إمّا is used, the subsequent 'or' can be represented by وإمّا.

§5 : 7. أى marks what follows it as an explanation of what precedes it,
corresponding to 'that is to say / namely / i.e.': مؤرّخ مصر المَشْهُور
أى المقريزىّ 'the famous historian of Egypt, namely Maqrīzī'.

§5 : 8. In contemporary Arabic it is not uncommon to find two nouns
linked by و simultaneously annexed to the same entity-term: كُتُب
وقِصَص اليَهُود 'the books and stories of the Jews'. This was avoided
until quite recently, and earlier authors would write كتب اليهود وقصصهم.

6

THEMATIC SENTENCE FORMS AND NOUN CLAUSES

§6 : 1. Thematic sentence structures can be classified according to the nature of the predicate, which can be:

(i) a noun or adjective [§§2 : 2, 3], as in هذا صَعْب 'this is difficult'; هذه صعوبة 'this is a difficulty'.

(ii) a prepositional phrase [§2 : 9], as in الوزير فى البيت 'the minister is in the house'; فى هذا صعوبة 'there is a difficulty in this' [§2 : 12].

(iii) a clause in verbal sentence structure [§3 : 2], as in الاميرة ماتت 'the princess died'; الاميرة ماتت أمها 'the princess' mother died'.

(iv) a secondary, emboxed, thematic sentence structure, as in هذه السياسة نتائجها نافعة [§2 : 7]سليمن هو الملك 'Solomon is the king', or in 'the results of this policy are advantageous', where the primary theme is 'this policy', while the predicate stated about it has the form of a clause consisting of a secondary theme ('its results') plus predicate ('are advantageous').

§6 : 2. In connection with thematic sentences with clause predicates [§6 : 1 (iii, iv)], it must be re-emphasized that the pronoun, in the predicate clause, referring to the theme, can occupy any position within that clause [§3 : 3]. In particular, when that pronoun functions as direct object of the verb, English idiom requires the verb to be turned into the 'to be . . .-ed by' structure: if the theme is 'this mosque' and the predicate stated about it is 'Umar built it', then the Arabic structure هذا المَسْجِد بناه عمر requires to be rendered idiomatically in English by 'this mosque was built by Umar'.

§6 : 3. In the examples cited hitherto, the theme has been simply enunciated. But it is also possible to place in front of a thematic sentence structure one of a set of functional words:

(i) إنَّ, which perhaps had, in the pre-history of Arabic, the sense of 'behold' (and the Biblical 'behold the lilies of the field, they toil not'

reproduces precisely the structure of an Arabic thematic sentence introduced by إنّ). It is for this reason that, when the theme is a pronoun, the
latter has the same form as a pronoun which functions as direct object of
a verb [§3 : 25]. Parallel to هى جميلة 'she is beautiful' one finds also
إنّها جميلة. The pronouns 'I' and 'we' after إنّ have either the expected
forms إنّنا إنّنى or abbreviated forms إنّا إنّى. However, any special
emphasis which might once have resided in the use of إنّ has been completely lost in standard Arabic prose, and it cannot be said that إنّها جميلة
differs at all, in sense or emphasis, from هى جميلة. When إنّ is employed,
the boundary between theme and predicate can optionally be marked by
la-: إنّ جواب هذا لصعب 'the answer to this is difficult'; إنّ فى هذا
لصعوبة 'there is a difficulty in this'.

(ii) ولكنّ لكنّ are expanded forms of إنّ and require to be
followed by a thematic sentence structure in which the theme, if a
pronoun, has the same form as after إنّ; like لكن [§5 : 4] they imply a
fairly strong antithesis, 'but (emphatic)/nevertheless'.

(iii) أمّا prefixed to a theme gives to it a certain degree of emphasis,
and can be roughly equated with English 'as for'. After أمّا the beginning
of the predicate is marked by ف: أما هذا فصعب 'as for this, it is difficult'.
But أما does not impart to a pronoun theme the object form as إنّ does:
hence, أما نحن فسياستنا واضحة 'as for us, our policy is plain'.

§6 : 4. Two further words resemble those described above, in that
they immediately precede the theme of a thematic sentence structure, but
they have an additional function in modifying the sense of the proposition
stated in the sentence; both of them entail direct object status for the
theme:

(i) لعلّ adds an idea of dubiousness to the proposition: لعله صحيح
'perhaps it is correct'*.

(ii) يا ليت/لَيْتَ converts the proposition into an aspiration instead

---

*This functional is also sometimes placed before a clause implying a hope or fear, e.g. 'in
the hope that perhaps . . .', 'for fear that perhaps . . .'.

of a statement: ليته مات قبل هذا ;'would that he were with us' يا ليته معنا معناه
'would that he had died before this'.

§6 : 5. Noun clauses are marked as such by having أَنَّ or أَنْ placed
before them. أَنَّ is followed by a thematic sentence structure, and
resembles إنَّ in giving a pronoun theme the form of a direct object
pronoun [§3 : 25]; أَنْ is followed by a verbal sentence structure. There are
thus three possibilities: (i) أَنَّ plus theme; (ii) أَنْ plus perfect verb;
(iii) أَنْ plus imperfect verb. The differentiation between these three
types of noun clause is that (i) and (ii) present the proposition stated in
the clause as a fact, whereas (iii) presents it as a conceptual proposition
not necessarily realized in fact, such as an aspiration, possibility etc.
Hence,

(i) أَيْقَنْتُ أَنَّ هذا صحيح 'I have become convinced (of the fact)
that this is correct'.

(ii) اتَّفَقَ أَنْ وَصَلَ الامير فى ذلك اليوم 'it happened that the
prince (in fact) arrived on that day'.

(iii) يُمْكِن أَنْ يصحّ هذا 'it is possible that this may be true'.

(iii and ii) أَمَلِى أَنْ تخبر الامير أنّنى ذهبت 'my hope is that you
may tell the prince that I have gone'.

§6 : 6. Noun clauses may be placed, like any other entity-term, after a
preposition: وَقَعَ هذا بَعْدَ أَنْ ذهبت 'this occurred after I had gone'
(equivalent to 'after my departure'). Nevertheless, when an أَنْ clause
functions as indirect object of a verb, it is not uncommon to omit the
preposition: in spite of the fact that the verb رَغِبَ in the sense of 'wish'
requires an indirect object with فى, and the preposition is indispensable
for the meaning when the object is a noun, pronoun or demonstrative, as
in رغب فى ذَهابى 'he wished for my departure', yet one may find
رغب أَنْ أذهب 'he wished that I would go'. Similarly, ذلك أَنَّ is
commonly used rather than ذلك لأَنَّ for 'that is because'.

§6 : 7. Theoretically, a noun-clause can in every case be replaced by a
verbal abstract, and *vice versa*. There are, however, idiomatic preferences

for one or the other structure, though these preferences do not coincide with English preferences. Hence an Arabic verbal abstract formulation will often need to be idiomatically rendered in English by a noun-clause structure with 'that'; or an Arabic noun-clause structure by the English verbal abstract 'to do so-and-so', as in e.g. يتعسّر علينا أن نذهب which is better rendered in English by 'it is impossible for us to go' than by the structure (felt in English to be more cumbrous) 'it is impossible for us that we should go'.

§6 : 8. The differentiation between factual and conceptual noun clauses is of special significance in two idioms common in modern Arabic, involving the use of a noun clause after إلّا 'except/apart from' and على 'on'. إلّا أنّ is analysable as 'apart from the fact that', and على أنّ 'on top of the fact that,' and both these forms should be rendered idiomatically in English by 'Nevertheless'. إلّا أنْ followed by an imperfect verb is analysable as 'apart from the supposition that', and corresponds idiomatically to 'unless'; على أنْ followed by an imperfect verb as 'on the supposition that' and corresponds to 'provided that'. Hence:

إلّا أنّ سياستنا تنجح
على أنّ سياستنا تنجح 'Nevertheless, our policy is succeeding'

إلّا أنْ تنجح سياستنا 'unless our policy succeeds'

على أنْ تنجح سياستنا 'provided that our policy succeeds'

§6 : 9. There exists an alternative structure to the use of a noun clause after verbs denoting activities of the mind, such as thinking, believing etc., and the verb رأى 'see' when the 'seeing' is a mental activity and not a physical one. A similar alternation exists in English between the expressions 'I believe that this is correct' and 'I believe this to be correct'. In Arabic, the proposition which is thought is expressed in the form of a thematic structure, of which the theme functions as direct object of the verb denoting thought, while its predicate may have any of the four types of predicate structure described in §6 : 1. Parallel, therefore to the noun-clause structures

نعتقد أنّ هذه السياسة نافعة 'we believe that this policy is useful'

أظنّ أنّك على الصّواب 'I think that you are in the right'

وجدَتْ أنّهم قد ذهبوا 'she discovered that they had gone'

the alternative structures are expressed as follows:

نعتقد هذه السياسة نافعة 'we believe this policy to be useful'

أظنّك على الصواب 'I think you to be in the right'

وجدتهم قد ذهبوا 'she discovered them to have gone'

§6 : 10. English sometimes uses 'it' referring forward to an entity-term occurring later in the sentence, as in 'it is possible that we may go', where 'it' is definable as the proposition 'that we may go', since this is the concept about which the predicate 'is possible' is stated. Arabic uses the corresponding pronoun in the same way, when a thematic sentence structure is required. While it is possible to write simply يمكن أن نذهب where the noun-clause functions as clarificatory entity-term explaining the pronoun implied in the verb form يمكن, yet if it is desired to begin the sentence with إنَّ (which requires a thematic sentence structure after it), one will find إنَّه يمكن أن نذهب. In addition, there are instances where the Arabic writer finds it inconvenient, for stylistic or rhetorical reasons, to accord his theme the first place in the sentence, and desires to postpone it to later in the sentence: in such cases, this pronoun serves as a generalized surrogate, at the beginning of the sentence, for the true theme which receives its overt expression later. Often, this usage is not reproduceable in English, and the pronoun must be left untranslated: e.g.,

أعتقد أنَّه يُحاوِل هذا كل الكتّاب الذين فيهم هِمَم عالية وآمال بَعيدة فى التقَدُّم 'I believe that all writers, in whom there are lofty ambitions and far-reaching hopes of progress, attempt this'.

MODIFICATIONS OF THE THEMATIC SENTENCE

§7 : 1. The verb forms كَانُوا كُنْتُ كُنْتَ كُنْتَ كَانَتْ كَانَتْ كَانَ
تَكُون يُكُون and in the perfect [§3 : 14] كُنَّا كُنْتُنّ كُنْتُمْ كُنّ
etc. in the imperfect [§3 : 16] are capable of being a true predicate in the
sense of 'exist'. But this use is relatively rare, and in the great majority of
cases this verb is a functional term which adds to the basic thematic
sentence ideas of time and modality which the thematic sentence as such
does not convey [§2 : 20]. The theme of the basic thematic sentence then
becomes the theme of the verb كان, while the predicate may be in any of
the four standard forms [§6 : 1]. Given the basic thematic structure
سياسته نافعة 'his policy is useful', this can be modified by كان to produce

كانت سياسته نافعة   'his policy was useful'

ستكون سياسته نافعة   'his policy will be useful'

يَحْتَمِل أنْ تكون سياسته نافعة   'it is probable that his policy may
be useful'

and the basic thematic structure هى فى البيت 'she is in the house' can be
modified into كانت فى البيت 'she was in the house', يحتمل أنْ تكون
فى البيت 'it is probable that she may be in the house'.

§7 : 2. If the predicate is a verbal clause [§6 : 1 (iii)], the sentence as a
whole naturally possesses already some time indication, and the addition
of كان then modifies the time indication possessed by the predicate clause
verb, by conveying that the unmodified thematic proposition was in the
past a valid statement; the addition of يكون that it will be in the future, or
might be etc., a valid statement. The thematic structure الامير يذهب الى
بيتها فى العَشَاء 'the prince goes to her house in the evening', when
modified by the addition of كان, implies that this statement was valid in
the past, hence كان الامير يذهب الى بيتها فى العشاء 'the prince used to

go to her house in the evening'; the statement قد انصرف الامير 'the prince has departed', when shifted into the past, becomes كان الامير قد انصرف 'the prince had (at that time already) departed', when shifted into the future, becomes يحتمل أنْ يكون الامير قد انصرف 'it is probable that the prince will (by then) have departed'. With a secondary thematic structure as predicate [§6 : 1 (iv)], كانت سياسته نتائجها نافعة 'the results of his policy were useful'.

§7 : 3. لَسْتُمْ لَسْنَ لَيْسُوا لَسْتَ لَسْتِ لَسْتُ لَسْتَ لَيْسَتْ لَيْسَ لَسْنا لَسْتُنَّ are verb-forms (inasmuch as containing an implied pronoun) which modify the basic thematic sentence by negativing it, and behave like كان. But ليس has no differentiation between perfect and imperfect, and therefore cannot add anything except the bare negative idea (if it is desired also to add any concepts of time or modality, كان is used with one of the negatives described in chapter 9). Thus,

ليست هذه السياسة نافعة	'this policy is not useful'
ليست فى البيت	'she is not in the house'
ليس الامير يذهب الى بيتها فى العشاء	'the prince is not in the habit of going to her house in the evening'
ليست سياسته نتائجها نافعة	'the results of his policy are not useful'

§7 : 4. A noun or adjective predicate of ليس can however be replaced by a prepositional phrase with *bi*: ليس هذا بعَجيب 'this is not astonishing', لستم بعُلَماء 'you are not learned men'.

§7 : 5. Certain other verbs, denoting the basic idea of 'being' with additional modifications, behave like كان, being capable of functioning either as true predicates, or as modifiers to a basic thematic sentence with the same structure as كان entails. Used in the latter way, one finds يُصْبِح أَصْبَح 'begin to be', يَظَلَّ ظَلَّ and يَدُوم دامَ 'continue to be', يَزال زال 'cease to be', يَكاد كادَ 'almost be', etc. Based on the thematic sentence الاخبار عنه شائعة 'the reports about him are current', one may find

كانت الأخبار عنه شائعة	'the reports about him were current'
دامت الأخبار عنه شائعة	'the reports about him continued to be current'
تُصبِح الأخبار عنه شائعة	'the reports about him are beginning to be current'
زالت الاخبار عنه شائعة	'the reports about him ceased to be current'

and based on هذا يذهب عن حفْظى 'this escapes my memory' one has كاد هذا يذهب عن حفظى 'this almost escaped my memory'.

§7 : 6. When employed as true predicates, دام and زال mean simply 'continue' and 'cease', and do not require an object, as in دامت المُحارَبة 'the fighting continued' زالت المحاربة 'the fighting ceased'. But كاد can be used as a true predicate in the sense 'be on the point of' followed by a noun-clause functioning as direct object, without however being differentiated in sense from the structure described in §7 : 5, hence in lieu of the expression there mentioned كاد هذا يذهب عن حفظى one may alternatively find كاد هذا أن يذهب عن حفظى.

§7 : 7. عاد يَعُود as a true predicate means 'return', as modifier of a thematic sentence 'be again/be once more': عادت المسألة موضوع بحث 'the problem was once again a subject of study'.

§7 : 8. جَعَلَ يَجْعَل (as a true predicate, 'make') is also used in the sense of 'begin to', but only when followed by an imperfect verb: جعل يعمل 'he began to work'.

§7 : 9. It has already been emphasized [§§3 : 3, 6 : 2] that the entity-term selected as the main theme of a communication is not necessarily identical with the agent of a verb which functions as predicate to that theme. 'The reports are reaching them' can be phrased either as الأخْبار تبلغهم or as إنّهم تبلغهم الأخبار, according to whether the principal topic of the communication is visualized as the reports or the recipients of the reports. It follows therefore that when such a communication is modified by the use of one of these functional verb-forms, the agent of the functional verb is not necessarily the same as the agent of the predicate verb; the above mentioned structures, when modified by أَصبح, will become أصبحت الأخبار تبلغهم and أصبحوا تبلغهم الأخبار respectively, though in both cases the substance of the communication is 'the reports began reaching them'.

8

VERBS OF VAGUE APPLICATION; PARTICIPLES

§8 : 1. The verb forms which have hitherto been discussed carry with them a specific mention of the agent, or 'doer' of the action: both أَخْبَرَنِى 'he (implying an already known individual) informed me' and أَخْبَرَنِى الوزير 'the minister informed me' are structures which state the identity of the informant, and are to that extent specific in their application. Parallel to these there exists a set of verb forms, distinguished by different vowel patterns, which do not state this identity but imply vaguely that 'someone or something unspecified' is the agent.

§8 : 2. Verbs of vague application are characterized throughout all verb types by a vowel sequence *u–i* in the perfect and *u–a* in the imperfect. Thus:

Type	Perfect	Imperfect
I	فُعِلَ	يُفْعَلَ
II	فُعِّلَ	يُفَعَّلَ
III	فُوعِلَ	يُفاعَلَ
IV	أُفْعِلَ	يُفْعَلَ
V	تُفُعِّلَ	يُتَفَعَّلَ
VI	تُفُوعِلَ	يُتَفاعَلَ
VII	انْفُعِلَ	يُنْفَعَلَ
VIII	افْتُعِلَ	يُفْتَعَلَ
X	اسْتُفْعِلَ	يُسْتَفْعَلَ

Forms of vague application of Type IX verbs do not exist. It will be noticed that the imperfect form of vague application of a Type IV verb is indistinguishable from that of a Type I verb.

§8 : 3. When the specific verb has a direct object, the corresponding verb of vague application varies in its form *as if* the direct object were the agent; the direct object functions in the sentence structure as a surrogate for the unmentioned agent. In this situation the verb form can be rendered by the English (so-called 'passive') 'to be . . .-ed' form: أَخْبَرَنِى 'he informed me' is parallelled by أُخْبِرْتُ 'I have been informed' (by someone unspecified).

§8 : 4. When the specific verb has only an indirect object, the latter remains unchanged after the corresponding verb of vague application, while the verb does *not* undergo any modifications adapting it to the nature of the object term, but retains invariably the masculine singular form (the structure being thus closely analogous with French 'on leur a écrit'). While it is in some cases possible to render this structure by an English passive form, as in قد يُسْتَغْنَى عن هذه الأمور 'these things may well be dispensed with', yet in other cases it may need a radical rephrasing in English:

Specific	رَضِىَ الوزير عنهم	'the minister was satisfied with them'
	نرغب فى نتائج	'we desire some results'
Vague	رُضِىَ عنهم	'satisfaction was felt with them'
	يُرْغَب فى نتائج	'there is a desire for some results'

§8 : 5. In the vague form of Type I verbs from roots having *w* or *y* as second consonant, the latter is merged in the perfect into *i* and in the imperfect into *ā*: root ق . و . ل, specific قال 'he said' يقول 'he says', vague قِيلَ 'it has been said', يُقَال 'it is said'. The form يقال followed by a surrogate agent is an idiomatic expression corresponding to English 'called' or 'named', as in إمرأة تُقَال لها فاطمة 'a woman named Fatima'.

§8 : 6. The participle is a recognizable word pattern which is primarily an entity-term associated with a verb, and connoting the agent of the verbal idea but without adding any other information about that agent. The participle form associated with the verb كتب يكتب means simply 'writer', that is, an entity definable solely by the statement 'he writes' or 'he has written' and carries no further information about the entity. Consequently, الكاتب is congruous in meaning with الذى كتب or مَن كتب 'the person who wrote/writes', and كاتب with الذى يكتب or من يكتب 'a person who has written/writes'.

§8 : 7. Participles associated with verbs of specific application have the patterns:

Imperf.	Part.	Imperf.	Part.
: يَفعل	فَاعِل	: يَتَفَاعَل	مُتَفَاعِل
: يُفَعِّل	مُفَعِّل	: يَنْفَعِل	مُنْفَعِل
: يُفاعِل	مُفاعِل	: يَفْتَعِل	مُفْتَعِل
: يُفْعِل	مُفْعِل	: يَفْعَلّ	مُفْعَلّ
: يَتَفَعّل	مُتَفَعّل	: يَسْتَفْعِل	مُسْتَفْعِل

§8 : 8. In the word pattern فاعِل from roots with *w* or *y* as second consonant, the second root consonant is replaced by *hamza*: from root ق . و . ل the فاعِل pattern is قائِل. Such forms are therefore indistinguishable from the فاعِل pattern from a root with *hamza* as second consonant, as in سائل (س . ء . ل) 'enquirer'.

§8 : 9. Participial word patterns have however secondary functions in addition to being entity-terms as described in §8 : 6. All of them can be freely used as adjectives; and a good many can also be employed as nouns with a specialized sense, not merely the generalized sense of the agent of the verb. For example, the verb جَمَع يَجْمَع (with an indirect object introduced by the preposition بَيْن) means 'he/it combined/gathered/united', and the corresponding participial pattern can be:

(i) an entity-term meaning simply 'something which unites', as in الجَامِع بين الأُمَم 'the thing which unites the nations'; or

(ii) an adjective, as in قَوْل جامع بين العِتاب والعُطُوفة 'a speech combining reproach and sympathy'; or

(iii) a noun with the specialized sense 'mosque', as in فى هذه المدينة جامِع جميل 'there is a handsome mosque in this town'.

§8 : 10. An undefined participial pattern sometimes functions as clarificatory noun to the agent pronoun contained in the associated verb; but since the participle adds nothing to the sense of the verb, such structures are congruous in meaning with the use of a verb of vague application: أَخْبَرَنِى مُخْبِرٌ 'an informant informed me' is a communication stating no more than أُخْبِرْتُ 'somebody informed me/I was informed'.

§8 : 11. Participles associated with verbs of vague application have the patterns:

Verb	Participle	Verb	Participle
يُفْعَلُ (فُعِلَ)	مَفْعُولُ	يُتَفاعَلُ	مُتَفاعَلُ
يُفْعَلُ	مُفْعَلُ	يُنْفَعَلُ	مُنْفَعَلُ
يُفاعَلُ	مُفاعَلُ	يُفْتَعَلُ	مُفْتَعَلُ
يُفْعَلُ (أُفْعِلَ)	مُفْعَلُ	يُسْتَفْعَلُ	مُسْتَفْعَلُ
يُتَفَعَّلُ	مُتَفَعَّلُ		

§8 : 12. The structures involving the use of these patterns need careful attention, as they are sometimes of a nature very unfamiliar to users of European languages. On the basis of what has been said [§8 : 6], it will be appreciated that مَكْتُوب is congruous in sense with ما يُكْتَب 'a thing which somebody writes' or 'something in writing'; and can also have [§8 : 9] secondary functions, as an adjective as in إِفادة مكتوبة 'a written communication', and as a noun with the specialized sense 'letter'.

§8 : 13. This principle extends to the verb of vague application which has only an indirect object. On the basis of the structure يُرْغَب فى هذا 'there is a desire for this', there arises the clause structure ما يُرْغَب فيه 'a thing for which there is a desire', and this generates the participial structure مرغوب فيه which, when functioning as an entity-term, has the same sense as the clause structure.

§8 : 14. The adjectival use of the participle associated with a verb of vague application is modelled closely on the verbal use, to the extent that, just as the verb of vague application with an indirect object does not undergo modification adapting it to the nature of a feminine object term [§8 : 4], so in the participial structure generated therefrom the participle does not take a feminine form even when the noun which it qualifies or to which it serves as predicate is feminine or plural. The following examples, showing how the participial structures are generated, should be carefully studied:

(i) direct object structures

طلبنا هذه النتائج   'we sought these results'

تُطْلَب هذه النتائج   'these results are being sought'

هذه النتائج التى تطلب   'these results which are sought'

هذه النتائج المطلوبة   'these sought-for results'

(ii) indirect object structures

رغبنا فى هذه النتائج   'we desired these results'

يُرْغَب فى هذه النتائج   'there is a desire for these results'

هذه النتائج التى يُرْغَب فيها   'these results for which there is a desire'

هذه النتائج المرغوب فيها   'these desirable results'

§8 : 15. The parallelism between participial structure and qualifying clause structure is carried further than this. In English, a qualifying clause can be rephrased as a participle structure only provided that the agent of the verb in the clause is identical with the qualified noun, as is the case with 'the policy which coordinates our actions' which can be rephrased as 'the policy coordinating our actions'. This limitation is not present in Arabic, and in principle any qualifying clause can be rephrased as a participial structure even when the clause has a verb with an agent different from the qualified noun. Here again, we encounter the feature that the form of the participle is modelled on the form of the verb in the clause structure, and is not adapted to the nature of the noun qualified by the participle. Contrast therefore

المَوْضُوع الذى تشيع عنه الأخبار   'the subject about which the reports
الموضوع الشائعة عنه الاخبار   are current'

with

السياسة التى يشيع عنها الخبر   'the policy about which the report
السياسة الشائع عنها الخبر   is current'

§8 : 16. Inasmuch as every adjective has a corresponding verb, the structure described in the preceding paragraph is equally applicable to adjectives other than those of a participial pattern. Hence,

هذه المسألة التى يصعب تحليلها   'this problem of which the solution
هذه المسألة الصعب تحليلها   is difficult'

§8 : 17. The structures described in §§8 : 15, 16, hitherto exemplified by defined instances, are also applicable to the undefined adjective or participle:

هذا موضوع شائعة عنه الأخبار   'this is a subject about which the reports are current'

هذه مسألة صعب تحليلها   'this is a problem of which the solution is difficult'

§8 : 18. Since the differentiation between a verb of specific application and one of vague application very often resides simply in a difference of short vowels, the beginner reading unvocalized material will often face a problem in deciding which is intended. Here again (as with the case of the ambiguity over the status of a prepositional phrase mentioned in §2 : 11) the overall structure of the sentence is the deciding factor. When a verb is of such a nature that it implies the participation of two entities, then it can only have a specific application if either the sentence itself or the context in which it is placed mentions two entities: if mention is made of only one, then the reader must assume that the other entity is unmentioned and that the verb is a form of vague application. Take the following example:

قتل بعضهم اللُصُوص الذين هجموا على القَرْية فى تلك اللَيْـلـة

mentions two entities, and the verb is therefore of specific application, and the sentence is capable (according to contextual likelihood) of standing for either 'the robbers who attacked the village on that night killed some of them' or 'some of them killed the robbers who attacked the village on that night'; but if قتل بعضهم is a complete sentence, then it may represent 'he killed some of them' provided that the context suggests the participation of a previously mentioned 'he' in the action, but if this is not so then the verb must be assumed to be of vague application, and the statement represents 'some of them were killed'.

9

NEGATIVES

§9 : 1. One form of negativing a proposition has been mentioned above [§7 : 3], but there are a number of other negative functionals. ما is used to negative factual propositions, and is hence the appropriate negative for the perfect, particularly when used as a narrative form, as in ما كتب 'he did not write'; and for the imperfect when this denotes the immediate present, as in ما أكتب 'I am not at the moment writing'. لا is used to negative general or conceptual propositions, and is therefore appropriate for the imperfect denoting future time, or the durative or habitual present, or any of its modal aspects, as in لا يكتب 'he does not (habitually) write', 'he will/should/might/may/could/cannot write'.

§9 : 2. أن combined with لا is often written as ألا: يَجِب ألا نُغْفِل هذا 'it is necessary that we should not neglect this'.

§9 : 3. ما can also be used to negative propositions in the basic thematic structure, and, like ليس [§7 : 4], it *can* be followed by a noun or adjective predicate with the preposition *bi*: ما هذه سياستنا or ما هذه بسياستنا 'this is not our policy'.

§9 : 4. The negative لَم is always followed immediately by an imperfect verb, which then assumes the range of meaning otherwise associated with the perfect; the sense implied is very commonly that of a perfect employed as a descriptive form [§3 : 22]. Hence the negative of قد ذهب 'he has gone' is commonly لم يذهب 'he has not gone'.

§9 : 5. لا is also used with an immediately following noun, together with which it constitutes a sentence structure, having the sense 'there is no . . .': لا شَكّ في هذا 'there is no doubt about this'. A common instance of this usage is the expression لا بُد 'there is no avoidance', employed idiomatically for English 'inevitably': هذا نعترف لا بد إنّنا 'we inevitably admit this'. As is the case with the basic thematic sentence [§2 : 20], this structure has no inherent time limitation.

§9 : 6. Another common usage is that of إلّا 'except' after a negative, and such sentences are sometimes best rendered in English by the affirmative form with 'only': لا أَعْلَم إلّا هذا 'I know only this'.

§9 : 7. Negatived forms of كاد [§7 : 5] are also idiomatic; they connote strictly 'almost not', but should be rendered in English by the affirmative form with 'hardly': لا نكاد نَفْهَم هذا 'we hardly understand this'. Negatived forms of عاد [§7 : 7] imply 'no longer': ما عاد يزورنى 'he no longer visited me'.

§9 : 8. غَيْر is essentially a noun used normally in annexion to a noun or adjective, and has the sense of 'other than', but the following usages should be noted:

(i) when annexed to an adjective, it negatives the sense of the adjective. In older usage, the defined or undefined status of the phrase is marked by the presence or absence of the article with the adjective:

هذه المَسائل غير المهمّة   'these unimportant problems'

هذه المسائل غير مهمّة   'these problems are unimportant'

مسائل غير مهمّة   'some unimportant problems'

But many modern writers prefix the article to غير as well when it is required to have defined status:

هذه السُلْطة الغير المَحْدُودة   'this unlimited authority'

(ii) when annexed to a pronoun (with the form of a pronoun used as noun qualifier [§2 : 16]), it should be rendered 'other(s)' with omission of the pronoun:

هذه المسائل وغيرها   'these and other questions'

الوزير وغيره   'the minister and others'

(iii) when annexed to an undefined singular noun, it negatives the concept of unity implicit in the noun [§1 : 3], and must be rendered 'several': فى مَكان 'in one place'; فى غير مكان 'in several places'.

(iv) after a negative, it behaves like إلّا [§9 : 6]:

لا يعلم هذا غير الوزير   'only the minister knows this'

(v) when annexed to a noun clause introduced by أنْ it similarly has the same force as إلّا [§6 : 8], so that غير أنْ like إلّا أنْ means 'Nevertheless, . . .', 'However, . . .' or simply 'But, . . .'.

(vi) its use otherwise than annexed is virtually confined to the expression لا غير (or ليس غير)* placed after a proposition or phrase, and meaning 'solely': يعلم هذا لا غير 'he knows solely this'.

§9 : 9. غير annexed to any entity-term (otherwise than in the idiom described in §9 : 8 (iii) above) can be replaced by سِوَى:

نعتمد على سواهم 'we rely on others than them'

لا يعلم سوى ذلك 'he knows only that'

كلّ أحد سوى الامير 'everyone else than the prince'

§9 : 10. Arabic has no form corresponding structurally to English 'nobody', 'nothing', 'no (noun)' (apart from the structure described in §9 : 5), and sentences containing expressions of this nature are normally represented by the structure 'not . . . any . . .':

ما وجدنا فى هذا صعوبة 'we found no difficulty in this'

ما كتب الى احد 'he wrote to nobody'

لا يُشَوّشه شىء 'nothing troubles him'

Although the undefined noun is sufficient to express these senses, it is not uncommon to reinforce it after a negative by annexing to it أىّ or أيّة [§1 : 18]:

ما وجدنا فى هذا أيّة صعوبة 'we found no difficulty in this'

ليس هناك اىّ سبيل الى تحليل 'there is no way to a solution'

§9 : 11. The effect of this structural principle is specially noteworthy in cases where the negatived noun is a theme:

نعتقد أنّ ملكة لم تفعل كذلك 'we believe that no queen has ever acted thus'

§9 : 12. When one negative proposition has been propounded, a succeeding negative proposition may be begun with ولا irrespective of

---

*Both of them may have و prefixed to them.

the type of negative used in the first proposition; the second proposition can be either a full sentence, or can restate in modified form one element in the first sentence, leaving the remainder to be assumed to be identical in the two propositions: ما بَحَثْنا هذا ولا حاوَلْنا بَحْثَه 'we did not investigate this, nor did we attempt its investigation'; ليس الرجل فى البيت ولا المرأة 'the man is not in the house, nor is the woman';

هذا غير صحيح ولا عادِل   'this is untrue and unjust'

§9 : 13. The answer 'No!' to a question is لا, or more emphatically كَلّا 'No indeed!', 'certainly not!'.

§9 : 14. لا is also a generalized negative used to restate in modified form one element in a preceding proposition: اعتقدت هذا لا ذلك 'I believed this, not that'. Occasionally لَيْسَ may be encountered employed in a similar way: حَكَم على البلاد كلها ليس على العاصمة فَقَطْ 'he ruled over the whole country, not over the capital alone'. In modern Arabic there is a limited range of nouns and adjectives with which لا forms a compound word: لاسِلْكِـى 'wireless', لانِهائِـى 'interminable', لاشىء 'a nullity'. Quite common, however, is the insertion of لا between the preposition *bi* and its noun, in the sense 'without': بلا شك 'without doubt'.

§9 : 15. The verbal abstract عَدَم 'absence, non-existence' may be annexed to another verbal abstract with the function of negativing it: عدم إمكان هذا 'the impossibility of this'.

§9 : 16. لَنْ is an emphatic negative of the future: لن يذهب 'he will certainly not go'.

§9 : 17. قَطْ placed after a negative reinforces it in much the same way as does English 'at all': لا أعلم قط 'I do not know at all'.

10

INTENSIFIED ADJECTIVES AND SIMILAR WORD PATTERNS

§10 : 1. A word pattern أَفْعَل is often used as an adjective having an intensified sense 'particularly/specially so-and-so': parallel to the simple adjective سَرِيع 'speedy' there is أَسْرَع 'particularly speedy'; parallel to كَبِير there is أَكْبَر 'specially big'. Like other adjectives, these are capable of functioning as nouns [§1 : 21]. Except as described below [§10 : 8], this pattern has no differentiation between masculine and feminine, or between singular and plural.

§10 : 2. When the sentence contains an entity-term used as a standard of comparison expressed by the use of the preposition مِن (which in this case is equivalent to 'in relation to'), the intensified adjective must be rendered in English by the 'more . . .' or '-er' form: كتاب أكبر من هذا 'a bigger book than this'; هو أعرف بهذا منّا 'he is more acquainted with this than we are'. This may also be the case in contexts where a standard of comparison is clearly implied even if not overtly stated.

§10 : 3. When an intensified word-pattern of this kind functions as a noun annexed to an entity-term describing a category within which the noun alluded to by the intensified pattern is included, then the intensified word pattern must be rendered by 'most . . .' or '-est' forms in English. Two possible structures occur in this case, the first being that in which the category term is a defined plural: هذا أكبر كتبه 'this is the biggest of his books'; هو أعرفنا بهذا 'he is the best acquainted of us with this'.

§10 : 4. An alternative to this structure is one in which the category term is expressed by an undefined singular: أصعب مُشْكِلة لاقيناها 'the most difficult problem which we have encountered'; أنبل ملك فى العالم 'the noblest king in the world'.

§10 : 5. When an intensified word pattern is annexed to a defined singular, it signifies 'the . . .-est part of'. Hence, whereas أسفل المدن

[§10 : 3] and أَسْفَل مدينة [§10 : 4] both imply 'the lowest town [among a group of other towns]', the sense of أَسْفَل المدينة is 'the lowest part of the town'.

§10 : 6. The category term can also be represented by a clause beginning with مَن or ما [§4 : 6]: أَجمل ما رأيت 'the most beautiful thing I have seen', أَجمل مَن رأيت 'the handsomest person I have seen'. Such expressions can then be further particularized by the addition of an explicit category noun in the defined plural introduced by the preposition مِن: أَجمل ما رأيت من المَناظِر 'the most beautiful sight I have seen'; أَجمل مَن رأيت من المَشايِخ 'the handsomest shaikh I have seen'. These latter structures are consequently congruous in sense with اجمل مَنْظَر رأيت and اجمل شيخ رأيت.

§10 : 7. When there is no standard of comparison expressed or implied, and no category term expressed or implied, the intensified adjective form must be rendered by 'very . . .' or by the simple unqualified adjective in English: الشيخ الأَعلم 'the very learned shaikh'; الصدر الأَعظم 'the Grand Vizier'; الموضوع الأَهَمّ 'the really important subject'. This is the case with certain adjectival notions which are expressed in Arabic *only* by the intensified form, such as أَوْسَط 'middle'.

§10 : 8. Traditional, and to a large extent modern, prose usage requires that the intensified adjective form should *only* exhibit differentiation between masculine and feminine, singular and plural, when it has *itself* the article. If this is not the case, then only the context will reveal whether its implications are masculine or feminine, singular or plural: هم أَكرم الناس 'they are the most generous of men'; هى أَجمل مدينة رأيتها 'it is the most beautiful city I have seen'; هؤلاء أَجمل النساء 'these are the most beautiful of women'. When it has the article, it is differentiated according to the following patterns:

	Masculine	Feminine
Singular	الأَفْعَل	الفُعْلَى
Plural	الأَفاعِل	الفُعَل

though there are a few such adjectives which have a masculine plural of a different pattern to be described later [§13 : 4]. Thus, الشَّرْق الأَوْسَط 'the Middle East', but القُرُون الوُسْطَى 'the Middle Ages'.

§10 : 9. Instances where this principle is controverted will, however, occasionally be encountered: الطائرات الأَسرع من الصوت 'supersonic aircraft', and conversely دول كُبْرَى وصُغْرَى 'great and small states'.

§10 : 10. A noun which qualifies [§1 : 19] an intensified adjective has the undefined form, thus contrasting with the structure involving a simple adjective. Further, the adjective is in this case *not* formally annexed to the noun, from which it follows that the noun need not immediately follow the adjective. In fact, there is a fairly strong tendency to place the qualifying noun in this structure right at the end of the sentence. The simple adjective structure هو واسع المعرفة بهذه المسائل 'he is widely acquainted with these problems' contrasts with هو أُوسع منّا بهذه المسائل معرفة 'he is more widely acquainted than us with these problems'. English idiom will often require sentences of this nature to be recast: كان الملك أشدّ من الوزير فى تحصيل هذه النتائج رغبة 'the king wished more fervently than the minister to achieve these results'.

§10 : 11. خَيَـْر 'good' and شَرّ 'bad' are basically nouns, as in نطلب الخير 'we seek the good', but are often incorporated into the same structures as intensified adjective forms: thus, هذا خير من ذلك 'this is a better thing than that'; شرّهم 'the worst of them'.

§10 : 12. أوَّل 'first' and آخِر 'last' are also intensified adjectives (though slightly irregular in pattern) and occur in the annexion structures described §§10 : 3, 4: أوّل أمر حاوله 'the first thing which he attempted'; لأوّل مَرّة 'for the first time'; آخر ليلة من الشهر 'the last night of the month'; آخر أبْواب الكتاب 'the last of the book's chapters'; but [§10 : 5] أوّل اليوم 'the first part of the day'; آخر الأمر 'the end of the matter'.

§10 : 13. The pattern ما أفْعَلَ followed by an entity-term which has the status of a direct object constitutes an exclamatory sentence structure implying surprise or admiration: ما أَجْهَلَكُم 'how ignorant you are!'; ما أَفضل هذا 'how excellent this is!'.

§10 : 14. The pattern أَفْعَل is also found in adjectives denoting colours and certain other physical qualities; this pattern has a feminine singular فَعْلاء and a plural (masculine and feminine) فُعْل: الكتـاب الأَحْمَر 'the red book'; راية حَمْراء 'a red flag'; عُرْج 'lame (people)'.

11

CIRCUMSTANCE CLAUSES

§11 : 1. A 'circumstance' clause has the primary function of describing a situation which is represented as simply an attendant circumstance to the main statement; and it may have one of three possible structures: (i) it may begin immediately with an imperfect verb, or (ii) it may begin with وَقَدْ followed by a perfect verb, or (if negative) with وَلَمْ and an imperfect verb, or (iii) it may begin with و plus a thematic structure.

§11 : 2. A circumstance clause of type (i) may either describe a situation existing simultaneously with that of the main statement, or an intention present at that time: خرج يحمل الكتاب فى يده 'he went out carrying the book in his hand'; ذهب الى عمان يُخْبِر الملك بالأخبار 'he went to Amman with the intention of informing the king of the news'. In type (ii) the situation is anterior in time to the main statement, and in type (iii) contemporaneous with it: جَرَتْ هذه الوَقائِع وقد زالت الحرب 'these events occurred when the war had ceased'; جرت هذه الوقائع والحرب قائمة 'these events occurred while the war was going on'.

§11 : 3. The purely temporal implications of a circumstance clause may, however, have added to them a logical significance which may be either causal ('inasmuch as') or antithetical ('although'). It is therefore important to recognize such a clause, and to appreciate that و is not in these cases a connective [§5 : 2] and should not be translated 'and'. Clauses of types (ii) and (iii) can often be recognized by the fact that the presence of قد or the thematic structure interrupts a sequence of sentences beginning with a narrative perfect verb: انصرف الوزير وقد فَرِغَ من شُغْلِه فمضى الى عمان 'the minister, inasmuch as he had now finished his work, departed and proceeded to Amman'; انتخبوه وهو غائِب عن البلاد فى ذلك الوقت فزالت المقاومة كلها 'they elected him, although he was at that time absent from the country, and all opposition ceased'.

§11 : 4. The formal criterion distinguishing a circumstance clause of type (i) from a qualifying clause is that the latter can only be introduced without the functional which marks it as such when the qualified noun is undefined [§4 : 1, 3]; whereas the entity-term whose situation is described by a circumstance clause is regularly defined.

§11 : 5. A circumstance clause beginning with و will sometimes be found treated functionally as a theme phrase introduced by أمّا [§6 : 3 (iii)]: أمّا وقد فرغنا من هذا فيَـجِب أنْ نفكّر فى أمر آخَر 'inasmuch as we have now finished with this, we must consider another matter'.

§11 : 6. An idiom which deserves some remark is the use of a circumstance clause beginning with و after a phrase which has not got the formal structure of a sentence, but may be felt to be equivalent in sense to one. Instead of the structure, of a formal sentence with circumstance clause attached, مَضَتْ مُدّة ونحن نَهْتَمّ بهذا المَشرُوع 'some time has passed while we have been concerning ourselves with this project', one may encounter مُنْذُ مدّة ونحن نهتم بهذا المشروع 'for some time past we have been concerning ourselves with this project'.

12

CONDITIONAL SENTENCES AND SIMILAR STRUCTURES

§12 : 1. Conditional sentences have a characteristic structure in that a perfect verb at the beginning of either of the two component clauses changes its normal implications to those of an imperfect, and will therefore have to be rendered by an English present in the conditioning clause, and by a present or future in the conditioned one, unless the context is such that an imperfect would, without the presence of a conditioning clause, have referred to past time [§3 : 19 (ii)]. The principal functionals which mark a conditioning clause are إِنْ and إِذَا 'if':

إن سألتموه أجاب   'if you ask him, he will reply'

إذا فكّرنا فى هذا رأينا حقيقته   'if we think about this, we see the truth of it'

On the other hand, if the context is such that يشاورهم would, unconditioned, have implied 'he used to consult them', this will generate the conditional structure اذا اقْتَضَت الحال شاورهم 'if the situation demanded, he used to consult them'. In the conditioning clause, the only alternative to the verbal sentence-structure is a rather rare one in thematic sentence structure with إِنْ followed by a pronoun theme: إن انتم سألتموه 'if you ask him'. In the conditioned clause, however, any other type of sentence structure can and frequently does occur, provided that it is marked as a conditioned one by having ف placed before it:

إن فعلوا كذا كانت أغراضهم واضحة   'if they act thus, their motives will be obvious'
إن فعلوا كذا فأغراضهم واضحة

§12 : 2. The use of the perfect verb form كان followed by a perfect verb predicate serves to site a conditioning clause in past time: إن كان الوزير قال هذا فقد أخطأ 'if the minister did say this, he made a mistake' (to be analysed as 'if it *is* the case that the minister said this', see §7 : 2).

83

§12 : 3. Since لَمْ with an imperfect is equivalent to a negatived perfect [§9 : 4], this form in a conditional sentence undergoes the same shift in meaning as the affirmative perfect: إن لم تكتب لم يذهب 'if you do not write, he will not go'.

§12 : 4. إذا with the conditional structure can also have the sense of 'when' (referring to the future) or 'whenever': إذا انصرف اخبرتك بالحقيقة 'when he departs, I will tell you the truth'; اذا سمعنا هذا وجب علينا أن نرفضه 'whenever we hear this, we ought to reject it'. Other functionals are also used with the conditional structure, the most important being أيْنَمَا مَهْمَا 'if ... anything/whatever', مَنْ 'if ... anybody/whoever', 'where-ever', كُلَّمَا 'whenever/as often as':

من قال هذا فالاستنتاج واضح	'if anyone says this, the inference is obvious'
مهما قال لم أصدّقه	'whatever he says, I will not believe him'
مهما كان من الامر	'whatever the case may be'
كلما حاولنا هذا وجدناه غير نافع	'whenever we attempt this, we find it useless'.

It should however be observed that some of these functionals, e.g. مَنْ and كلما, normally use the characteristic conditional structure only when the clause they introduce precedes the complementary clause; whereas if they come after the main clause, the perfect verb should be taken as alluding to past time: لم أصدّق من قال هذا 'I have never believed anyone who said this'; كانت فى أعماق الجزع كلما هبّت عليها ريح شُبْهة 'she was in the depths of despair every time a breath of doubt blew upon her'.

§12 : 5. A conditional structure introduced by كُلَّمَا and having an intensified adjective in the conditioned clause corresponds idiomatically to the English structure 'the more ... the more': كلما حاولنا وجدناه أيْسَر 'the more we try, the easier we find it'.

§12 : 6. ما followed by the conditional structure has the sense 'so long as': ما بَقِىَ هنا سَلِمَ 'so long as he stays here, he will be safe'.

§12 : 7. Hypothetical sentences also consist of two clauses, but present the conditioning proposition as a mere supposition, or a remote possibility, or as definitely invalid. These imply no time indication at all, and will have to be rendered in English in one of two ways only determinable by the context (examples below). The conditioning clause is introduced by لَو followed by a perfect verb, the conditioned one has a perfect verb which may or may not be introduced by la: لو كتبتَ اليه فعل ما تُريد 'supposing you were to write to him, he would do what you wish' or 'If you had written to him, he would have done what you wish'; لو أخبرتَه بهذا لكانت فيه مَتْفَعَة 'supposing that you were to inform him of this, there would be some advantage in it' or 'if you had informed him of this, there would have been some advantage in it'.

§12 : 8. A hypothesis sited in past time can, however, be made explicitly so by the use of كان with perfect verb predicate: لوكنتَ أخبرته means unambiguously 'if you had informed him'.

§12 : 9. In place of لو followed by a perfect verb, one may find لو أنَّ followed by a thematic structure: لو أنَّ الحرب تَدوم لَوَجَب علينا صرف مال كثير 'if the war were to continue, it would be necessary for us to spend much money'.

§12 : 10. لو can also be used, with the same structure as it has in a hypothetical conditioning clause, to introduce a complete sentence expressing an unfulfilled aspiration: 'if only I had known that!' لو علمتُ ذلك.

§12 : 11. The above-mentioned structure can also function as object of a verb of wishing: وَدَّ لو عَلِمَهُ 'he wished he had known it'.

§12 : 12. The negative of لو when it introduces a full clause structure is لو لم. The form لولا is prefixed to an entity-term with which it constitutes a quasi-clause, and must be rendered by 'had it not been for/ were it not for'. The conditioned clause then has the same structure as it would have had the preceding clause been fully expressed: لولا رغبة الملك

لَاَ عْتَزَلَ الوزير 'had it not been for the king's wish, the minister would have resigned' or 'were it not for the king's wish, the minister would resign'.

§12 : 13. وإلّا with the sense of 'otherwise' is an abbreviated form of a conditioning clause, and can be followed by a conditioned clause having the same structure as would follow a fully expressed clause implying 'if this is not so':

$$ علينا أنْ نفعل هذا وإلّا {بَطَلَتْ مُحاوَلتنا \atop فمحاولتنا تَبْطُل} $$

'we are obliged to do this, otherwise our effort will be frustrated'.

§12 : 14. وإنْ and وَلَوْ introduce anti-conditioning clauses which are normally placed after the main statement, or emboxed within its structure. The anti-conditional clause itself has the same structure as a conditional or hypothetical clause introduced by إنْ or لَوْ. In the case of وإن, the main statement does not have the conditioned structure with the distinctively conditional use of the perfect, but any part of it which comes after the anti-conditioning clause is normally introduced by ف. In the case of ولو the main statement does have the hypothetical main statement structure; consequently, the English translation of a perfect verb may have to be modified into the 'would' form in the light of a subsequent anti-conditioning clause:

تُقْنِعنا البَراهين على هذا وإن كانت قَليلة / البراهين على هذا وان كانت قليلة فتقنعنا	'the proofs of this, though they are few, convince us'
إنَّ هذا القول ولو كانت البراهين عليه مَعْدُومة لأَيْقَنْتُهُ / أيقنت هذا القول ولو كانت البراهين عليه معدومة	'I would be certain of this statement, even if the proofs of it were lacking'

§12 : 15. Sometimes, however, an anti-conditioning clause precedes its main statement in toto; in such cases it may be impossible by formal criteria to recognize the anti-conditional nature of the clause, and this can

only be determined by the context: قد حصل على غَرَض وإن لم يحصل
على غيره فذلك يُقْنِعه 'he has achieved one objective, and even if he
does not achieve anything else, that will satisfy him'.

§12 : 16. In modern style, it is common to prefix إلاّ أنّ or غير أنّ
or ولكن to the segment of a main statement which comes after an
anti-conditioning clause: الشيـخ وإن حَضَّنـا عـلى الرِفْتى بالنساء غير
أنّه مُسْتَهِين بهنّ 'the shaikh, although he urges us to treat women
gently, nevertheless is contemptuous of them'.

§12 : 17. There is a type of expression in which two antithetical
alternatives are posed, and the decision between them is said *not* to affect
the validity of the main statement; the English form for this is '(no
matter) whether . . . or . . .'. In Arabic, the first alternative is posed in
the form of a perfect verb structure *without* any introductory functional,
the second is introduced by أمْ or أوْ plus either another perfect verb
structure or some abbreviated structure restating only that part of the
second proposition which differs from the first:

عليك أنْ تذهب رَضِيتَ او   'you must go, whether you are
كَرِهْتَ   willing or unwilling'

يعترفه كلّهم بَحَثَ عن حقيقته   'every one of them admits it, no
أم لم يبحث   matter whether he has investi-
              gated its truth or has not'
              [§9 : 4]

هذا واجِب علينا رغبنا فيه أم لا   'this is our duty, whether we wish
              it or not' [§9 : 13].

§12 : 18. In such expressions, when the first alternative is in the form
of كان with an adjective predicate, it is usual to place the adjective in
front of the كان: قد نحصل على منفعة عظيمة كانت أم قليلة 'we may
achieve some benefit, whether it be great or small'.

13

TERMINAL VARIATIONS IN NOUNS AND ADJECTIVES

§13 : 1. Most nouns and adjectives, and all imperfect verbs, have a set of terminal variations, the choice between which is dictated by the function of the word in relation to the rest of the sentence. All these phenomena are together grouped under the name of إِعْرَاب. To a large extent, these phenomena are manifested only in short vowels at the end of the word, and to that extent are not apparent in unvowelled script, and hence can (and indeed must) be disregarded for the purpose of simply reading and comprehending Arabic as normally written. At the same time, there are cases where these phenomena do manifest themselves in the ordinarily written shape of the word, and it is therefore necessary to give an account both of the functional situations which govern the choice of إعراب, and of the variations in word pattern which they entail.

§13 : 2. There are three varieties of إِعْرَاب applicable to nouns and adjectives, and three applicable to imperfects. رَفْع is the name given to the short vowel termination -u which occurs in nouns, adjectives and imperfects, and also to other phenomena which occur in some words in functional situations which would in others require the short vowel -u. نَصْب is the name given to the short vowel termination -a in some words, and functionally parallel phenomena of another kind in others, and this likewise occurs in nouns, adjectives and imperfects. خَفْض or جَرّ is the name given to the short vowel termination -i, characteristic only of nouns and adjectives, and to other functionally parallel phenomena.

Also included under the heading of إِعْرَاب is a terminal -n added after the variable vowel in certain circumstances [§13 : 11].

§13 : 3. Besides the broken plural patterns of nouns (and some adjectives, §1 : 25), there is a plural pattern in which a masculine termination is added to the basic pattern of the singular, the latter remaining unchanged; this termination is also susceptible of إِعْرَاب variation, being -ūna for the رفع and -īna for the نصب and جَرّ. There is a parallel

feminine termination which is -ātu(n) for the رفع and -āti(n) for نصب
and جرّ, which replaces the -a(t) termination of the singular if this is
present, although a plural of this kind is in some cases found with words
of which the singular does not have it, such as إنتخاب 'election', إنتخابات
'elections'. And whereas this masculine plural termination always (with
one or two anomalous exceptions such as سنِينَ, سنِنُونَ 'years') alludes
to male persons, the feminine one is applicable to persons and things.

§13 : 4. The principal classes of word in which this type of plural
occurs are derived adjectival patterns ending in -iyy [§1 : 20] and participial patterns [§§8 : 7, 11]. Thus, for 'Egyptian' one has

fem. plur.	masc. plur.	fem. sing.	masc. sing.	
المصريّاتُ	المصريُّونَ	المصريّةُ	المِصْرِىُّ	رفع
المصريّاتِ	المصريّينَ	{ المصريّةَ / المصريّةِ	المصرىَّ / المصرىِّ	نصب / جرّ

In addition, a few of the intensified adjective patterns use a masculine
plural of this kind [§10 : 8], such as الأَكْثَرُونَ 'most people'.

§13 : 5. The choice of إعراب for a qualifying adjective is dictated by
the functional position (and hence the إعراب) of the noun it qualifies;
and the explanatory noun of a demonstrative [§2 : 1] has the إعراب which
is appropriate to the function of the demonstrative in the sentence.

§13 : 6. The functional situations requiring رفع of a noun or adjective
are when it is
  (a) the theme of a thematic sentence structure, except as mentioned
below [§13 : 8 (a)]; or
  (b) the agent of a verb of specific application, or surrogate agent of
a verb of vague application [§8 : 3]; or
  (c) the predicate in a thematic sentence structure, unless the latter is
modified as mentioned below [§13 : 8 (c, d)]; or
  (d) the agent of the verbal concept expressed by a participle or
adjective used in the structure described in §§8 : 15, 16.
  Hence, (a) الأَميرةُ قد ماتت أمّها 'the princess' mother has died',
(b) أُخْبِرَ الوزيرُ بهذا أخبرنى الوزيرُ بهذا 'the minister informed me of this';

بهذا 'the minister was informed of this', (c) هو الوزيرُ 'he is the minister', (d) مدينة كثير سكّانُها 'a city whose inhabitants are numerous'.

§13 : 7. The functional situations requiring جرّ are

(a) position immediately after a preposition;

(b) the function of qualifier to an annexed noun or adjective [§1 : 12, 19].

Thus, فى الدولة 'in the state', وزير الدولة 'the minister of state', فارغ الفهم 'devoid of understanding'.

§13 : 8. The scope of the use of the نصب is a good deal wider and more complex; besides situations to be described later, it occurs in

(a) a theme preceded by one of the functionals which impart object status to the theme [§§6 : 3, 4, 5]: إنّ الاميرة قد ماتت 'the princess has died'; لعلّ السياسيّين مُخْطِئُون 'perhaps the politicians are mistaken'.

(b) the direct object of a verb: شاورت السياسيين 'I consulted the politicians'.

(c) the predicate of a thematic sentence structure when this is modified in the manner described in §§7 : 3, 5: كانوا خارجين عن المُنَظَّمة 'they were outside the organization'. It is to be remarked that when a defined predicate is marked as such by the insertion of a pronoun [§2 : 7] after one of these modifying verbs, the resulting structure is treated in one of two alternative ways: the pronoun with the predicate may be treated as a clause form in which the predicate is as normal in the رفع form, as in كان العرب هم الغالبون, or the pronoun may be treated as a pure functional not affecting the structure of modifying verb plus predicate, as in كان العرب هم الغالبين 'the Arabs were the victors'.

(d) either theme or predicate of a proposition which is an object of thought [§6 : 9]: أعتقد السياسيّين مُخْطِئين 'I believe the politicians to be mistaken'.

§13 : 9. Nouns and adjectives ending in -ā are incapable of any terminal vowel variation: hence, هذا مَعْنَى القول 'this is the meaning of the speech', من معناه 'from its meaning' etc.

§13 : 10. Nouns and adjectives other than those mentioned in the preceding paragraph, when they are *neither* made defined by the addition of the article *nor* in annexed position, are divisible into two classes exhibiting different types of إعراب. One class, in these circumstances, has only two potentialities of إعراب variation, namely -*u* for the رفع and -*a* for both نصب and جرّ. This class is signalized in Wehr by a ². The principal types of noun and adjective belonging to this class are:

(*a*) those having the pattern أفْعَل or فَعْلاء.

(*b*) broken plurals of certain patterns, including among others those with the vocalic pattern *a* - *ā* - *i* or *a* - *ā* - *ī* or *a* - *ā* - *i* - *a(t)*;

(*c*) nouns of single application which are of non-Arabic origin;

(*d*) nouns of single application ending in ة, or referring to female persons even when not so ending.

Hence, وجه أسْوَدَ 'a negro's face'; فى أغْرَبَ من هذا 'in something stranger than this'; فى مَكاتِيبَ 'in some letters'; لتلامِذةَ 'for some pupils'; موت مُعاوِيةَ 'the death of Mu'āwiya'; قِصّةَ زَيْنَبَ 'the story of Zaynab'.

§13 : 11. All other nouns and adjectives (including a number of names of males, which are defined in themselves [§1 : 7] and are not made defined by the article) belong to the other class. These are characterized by the fact that, when neither defined by the article nor in annexed position, they have the full range of three terminal variations *and* automatically assume an -*n* after a variable short إعراب vowel; but this *n* is not reflected in the consonantal shape of the word [§S : 26], except in the case of the نصب termination -*a-n* which is marked by an added *alif*; nevertheless, this added *alif* is not used if the word ends in ة or in a *hamza* preceded by *ā*. Hence جاءَ رجلٌ 'a man came'; جاءَ رجلاً 'he came to a man'; جاءَ محمدٌ 'Muhammad came'; جاءَ محمداً 'he came to Muhammad'; فى مدينةً 'in a city'; جاءَ مدينةً 'he came to a city'; كَسَبَ جَزاءً 'he earned a great reward'; أخذ جُزْءاً منه 'he took a part of it'.

§13 : 12. Participle patterns listed in §8 : 7, when derived from roots having *w* or *y* as third consonant, together with verbal abstracts of Type V and VI verbs from such roots, have a special set of terminal

variations, exemplified as follows: the participle pattern فاعِل from root
ر . م . ى, and the verbal abstract pattern تَفَعُّل from root ج . ل . و, are:

	Undefined *and* unannexed	Defined *or* annexed
رفع and جرّ	رامٍ (ال)تَجَلٍّ تَجَلٍّ	(ال)تَجَلِّى (ال)رامِى
نصب	رامِيًا تَجَلِّيًا (ال)رامِىَ	(ال)تَجَلِّىَ

The same phenomenon is found in the broken plurals of certain nouns
where the pattern of the plural has *i* as its last vowel; such nouns are in
some cases derived from roots ending in *w* or *y*, as for example مَجْرًى
(root ج . ر . ى), with a plural exemplified in هذه مَجارٍ جديدةٌ 'these
are new courses' but هذه المَجارِى الجديدةُ 'these new courses'; in other
cases they are anomalous formations, such as the plurals of أرض and ريد,
exemplified in تلك هى أراضٍ 'those are distant lands'; تلك أراضٍ بعيدةٌ
الاسلام 'those are the lands of Islam'; لهن أيدٍ بَيَضاءُ 'they have white
hands'; أَيْدِيهِنَّ بيضاءُ 'their hands are white'.

§13 : 13. The nouns أب 'father' and أخ 'brother' when annexed assume
long vowel terminations showing the same kind of vowel variation as the
short vowel ones of other nouns: مات أبُو الامير 'the prince's father
died'; لَقِيتُ أبا الامير 'I met the prince's father'; كتبت الى أخِيه 'I wrote
to his brother'. The entity-term ذُو 'one possessed of' (used only in
annexed position) shows the same variation: هو ذو معرفةٍ بهذا 'he is
knowledgeable about this'; وجدت ذا معرفةٍ 'I found someone knowledgeable'; مِن ذى معرفةٍ 'from someone knowledgeable'. The feminine
of ذو, however, which is ذات, behaves like an ordinary noun: وجدتها
ذاتَ معرفةٍ بهذا 'I found her to be knowledgeable about this'.

§13 : 14. The addition of the qualifying pronoun form -ī [§2 : 16]
entails the disappearance of all the short vowel variable terminations, and
of the variable long vowels characterizing أب and أخ: بيتى 'my house'

and أُبِى 'my father' are invariable whatever their functional position in
the sentence.

§13 : 15. The masculine plural terminations described in §13 : 4 lose
their final syllable when they are in annexed position: هم ممثّلو فرنسا
'they are the representatives of France', بين سياسيّيهم 'among their
politicians'.

§13 : 16. After لا used in the sense of 'there is no . . .' [§9: 5], the noun
has the termination -a but without any additional -n; and since the
conventional spelling with *alif* [§13 : 11] explicitly represents the termination -a-n, this *alif* is not present in these cases, hence the spellings لا بُدَّ
etc.

§13 : 17. The use of the نصب also indicates an internal object. This is
in principle the verbal abstract of the verb to which it serves as object,
and it may either stand alone or be qualified in any way appropriate to a
noun; it can however be replaced by a different verbal abstract, or (if
qualified by an adjective) omitted altogether. The structures involving
the use of an internal object often require considerable recasting in order
to achieve an idiomatic English rendering. The following are some
characteristic examples.

فَرِحَ فَرَحًا	'he was overjoyed'
نبح الكلب نُباحًا عاليًا	'the dog barked loudly'
جرى سَعْيًا سريعًا/جرى سريعًا	'he ran swiftly'
ضَحِكَ ضَحْكَ المجنون	'he laughed like any madman'
تقدّم تقدُّمًا أَعْجَبَنَا	'he made progress in a manner astonishing to us'
لم يجتهد اجتهادَنا	'he has not striven as much as we have'

§13 : 18. The نصب further marks the predicate term in a structure
closely resembling that described in §6 : 9, which occurs after verbs
denoting the imparting of a new quality to an entity-term: جعلوه غَرَضَهم
'they made it their object'; انتخبوه نائبًا 'they elected him deputy'.

§13 : 19. An *undefined* نصب may be found

(*a*) denoting the motivation of an act: فعله تَدَيُّنَا 'he did it out of piety'*;

(*b*) as a substitute for the use of a circumstance clause [§§11 : 1–3]: انتخبوه وهو غائبٌ is equivalent in sense to انتخبوه غائبًا عن العاصمة عن العاصمة 'they elected him while (he was) absent from the capital'.

(*c*) marking a noun which qualifies an intensified adjective as described in §10 : 10.

§13 : 20. The إعراب of a participle or adjective used in the structure described in §§8 : 15, 16 is *not* dictated by its function in relation to its agent (although its masculine or feminine form is), but by its function in relation to the sentence. If it has a qualifying function, its إعراب follows that of the noun it qualifies; if it has a predicative function, it has رفع (or, in the circumstances described in §13 : 8 (*c, d*), نصب); or thirdly, it may be used in the undefined نصب in the manner described in §13 : 19 (*b*). Hence, قد نلاحظ هذا فى مدينة كثير سكّانُها 'we sometimes observe this in a populous city'; كانت روما مدينةً كثيرًا سكّانُها 'Rome was a populous city'; إنّ روما كثيرٌ سكّانُها 'Rome is populous'; حكم على المدينة مُتَمَرِّدًا سكّانُها 'he governed the city while its populace was in revolt'.

§13 : 21. Nouns denoting time or place often dispense with a preposition meaning 'in', 'at', 'during' etc., before them, and then have the نصب form: اتّفق يومًا 'it happened one day'.

---

*But a noun annexed to a defined term may be encountered used in this way provided that the definition is of the general character described in §1 : 1 (*b*): فَرَّ خَوْفَ المَوْتِ 'he fled for fear of death'.

14

TERMINAL VARIATIONS IN THE IMPERFECT

§14 : 1. The terminal variations of the imperfect verb can be divided into those affecting the forms where the agent pronoun is indicated by variations at the beginning of the word only, and those affecting the forms where the end of the word also reflects the agent pronoun. In the former set, the terminal variations are -*u* and -*a*, named respectively رفع and نصب (as are the same vowels when used in noun and adjective terminations), and absence of vowel, named جَزْم. In those forms of the imperfect in which the end of the word reflects the agent pronoun, the forms terminating in -*ūna* and -*īna* represent the رفع, while the نصب and جزم are alike characterized by omission of the syllable -*na* (and consequential adding of an *alif* after -*ū*, see §3 : 15); in those forms in which the termination is simply -*na* no terminal variation occurs at all. The رفع form of an imperfect occurs in all situations where there is no specific factor demanding نصب or جزم, as described below.

§14 : 2. Situations requiring نصب of the imperfect are

(i) when it is preceded by أنْ: أمرهم أن يخرجوا من العاصمة 'he commanded them to go away from the capital'.

(ii) when it is preceded by لِكَى/كَى 'in order to', or by *li*- when used in that sense: تأهّبوا لكى ينصرفوا/لينصرفوا 'they made preparations in order to depart'.

(iii) when it follows a negative proposition, or a query or a command or prohibition, and is introduced by ف having the sense of 'so as to'; this structure contrasts with the use of ف with a رفع which is a fresh factual statement, while the use of the نصب implies a theoretical consequence: كانوا لا يقرؤون الصحف فيكرهوا ما فيها 'they used not to read the newspapers so as to dislike what is in them' contrasts with كانوا لا

يقرؤون الصحف فيكرهون ما فيها 'they used not to read the newspapers, for they disliked what is in them'.

(iv) after certain senses of حَتَّى [§17 : 2 (i)].

(v) when it is preceded by the emphatic negative described in §9 : 16.

§14 : 3. Situations requiring جزم of the imperfect are

(i) when it is preceded by negative لَمْ [§9 : 4].

(ii) when it is preceded by لا in order to convey a prohibition: لا تَفْعَلْه (addressed to a man), لا تفعلوه (addressed to several people), لا تفعليه (addressed to a woman) 'don't do it'.

(iii) when it is preceded by li- or fal- used to convey an exhortation: فليعتبروا هذا 'let them then consider this'.

(iv) when it is used as a substitute for the conditional use of the perfect [§§12 : 1, 4, 5, 6, 14]: إن سألتموهم أجابوا = إن تسألوهم يُجيبوا 'if you ask them, they will reply'.

§14 : 4. The جزم of verbs from roots having the same letter as second and third consonants has forms which are now rarely used, it being in practice normal to employ the نصب form in lieu of the جزم in these cases: لم يَرُدَّ جوابًا 'he returned no answer'.

§14 : 5. The جزم of verbs from roots with w or y as second consonant, in those forms where the agent pronoun is reflected in changes at the beginning of the word only, has a short vowel in place of the long vowel into which the second root consonant is merged in رفع and نصب. Hence, beside يكون and يُريد, one finds لم يَكُنْ 'he was not' and لم يَرُدْ 'he did not wish'.

§14 : 6. In roots with w or y as third consonant, this may merge into the long vowel -ū or -ī in the رفع, while the نصب conforms to the standard pattern, hence أن يَجْرِيَ ,يَجْرِى; but if it merges into -ā the رفع is indistinguishable from the نصب, hence يَبْقَى ,يَبْقَى. In the جزم, the long vowel of the رفع is shortened, hence لم يَبْقَ ,لم يَجْرِ.

§14 : 7. These features of the جَزم are particularly troublesome to the beginner reading unvocalized texts, until he has a sufficient vocabulary to be able readily to select the sense appropriate to the context. A written form such as لم يرد may have to be interpreted as any of the following, according to the context:

لَمْ يَرُدَّ 'he did not return' (root (ر . د . د) [§§3 : 11, 14 : 4]

لَمْ يَرُدْ 'he did not wish' (root (ر . و . د) [§14 : 5]

لَمْ يَرْدَ 'he did not perish' (root (ر . د . ى) [§14 : 6]

لَمْ يَرِدْ 'he did not arrive' (root (و . ر . د) [§3 : 11]

15

PREPOSITIONAL PHRASES

§15 : 1. The importance of a prepositional phrase as indirect object of a verb, in defining the sense of the verb itself, has already been mentioned [§3 : 24]. One usage of general application deserves notice, connected with the proposition عَنْ. When this is used after a verb which has a sense equivalent to an adjectival predicate [§3 : 4], the adjective must in English be modified by the addition of 'too': ضَعُفَ عن محاربتهم 'he was too weak to fight them'.

§15 : 2. Prepositional phrases have also an important function as replacements for an annexion structure, particularly when the latter is (owing to its peculiar features described in §§1 : 12, 13) unsuitable. In principle, a verbal abstract or any other noun embodying a verbal concept can be annexed to an entity-term which represents either the theme pronoun of the verb or its direct object: beside the verbal sentence أَجابَهُ 'he answered him', the verbal abstract annexed to the pronoun إجابته may mean *either* 'the answer he gave' (with pronoun corresponding to the theme pronoun of the verb) *or* 'the answer given to him' (with pronoun corresponding to the direct object pronoun). But if it is desired to use the verbal abstract in e.g. the way described in §13 : 7 (i), which demands that it should be undefined, this structure is impossible, since annexion to the pronoun, which is a defined entity-term, makes the annexed word also defined [§1 : 13], and a prepositional phrase must be used in lieu. Similarly when it is desired to qualify a noun of any kind which requires to be undefined in sense, by a defined entity-term, the prepositional phrase replacement must be used instead of the annexion structure. Nor can a noun be annexed to two qualifying entity-terms if the nature of the qualification of each one is different: it is possible to write حُبّ المال والجاه 'the love of money and of rank', but in 'John's love of money', where the qualifier 'John's' corresponds to the theme of the verb in يحيى يُحِبّ المال 'John loves money' but the qualifier 'of money' corresponds to the direct object, then 'love' cannot be annexed to both.

§15 : 3. In all such situations, the annexion structure can be replaced by a prepositional phrase with ل or مِنْ. ل is used when the qualifying term represents either the direct object of the verbal idea, or a 'possessor' of the qualified noun (i.e. an entity which can be said to 'have' it in the widest range of senses); مِن is used when the qualifying term represents either the theme pronoun of a verbal idea, or an entity of which the qualified noun is a part. Hence,

(i) substitution for the direct object:

حُبّى لها 'my love of her'

تحليل لهذه الصعوبات 'a solution of these difficulties'

ابْتَسَمَ إجابةً لى 'he smiled by way of answering me' [§13 : 19(a)]

(ii) substitution for the 'possessor':

أَخٌ للامير 'a brother of the prince'

حَدٌّ بعيدٌ للبلاد 'a remote limit of the country'

(iii) substitution for the theme pronoun:

اعتقاد منّى 'a belief held by me'

قُلْتُ هذا رِضاءً منّى عن عَمَلِهِ 'I said this out of satisfaction on my part with his work'

(iv) part-whole relationship between the terms:

جُمْلة من أصْدِقاءِ الملك 'one group of the king's friends'

§15 : 4. In addition to the expedient described under §15 : 3 (iv) for handling expressions of the type 'an X of the Y', a common idiomatic structure is 'an X of (من) the Xs of Y', e.g.:

فى مَزْرَعةٍ من مَزارِعِ لُبْنانَ 'in a country district of the Lebanon'

§15 : 5. Where a structure consisting of annexed noun plus qualifying noun is followed by a qualifying adjective, it may not always be clear which of the two nouns the adjective is intended to qualify. This ambiguity can be resolved by replacing the annexion structure by a prepositional phrase with ل. The same is done in cases where the writer feels that the adjective belongs more closely with the noun it qualifies than does the noun qualifier (whereas the rules of annexion demand that the noun qualifier to an annexed noun must precede the adjective qualifier [§1 : 12]). Thus, المَرْحَلَة الأُولَى للمَعْرَكة means explicitly 'the first stage of the conflict', whereas مرحلة المعركة الاولى is ambiguous and could mean either that or 'the stage of the first conflict'. And although there is no formal ambiguity, one may well find, e.g. الغرض الأساسيّ لهذه السياسة 'the basic object of this policy' if the writer feels that 'basic object' is a more closely bound phrase than 'object of this policy'.

§15 : 6. A prepositional phrase with من can also be used as a substitute for a simple undefined noun: شرِبنا من الماءِ 'we drank some water', لا أرَى فى ذلك من صعوبةٍ 'I do not see any difficulty in that'. The undefined predicate adjective can be replaced by من with the defined adjective (the preposition then giving it an undefined sense), and this is specially common when, for structural reasons, such as length or complexity of the theme phrase, the predicate adjective precedes its logical theme: هذا القول ُ زائفٌ 'this statement is false', but من الزائفِ أنْ° نقولَ هذا 'it is false for us to say this' (logically equivalent to 'that we should say this, is a falsity'). And a very characteristic idiom is the use of من to give an explicitly undefined sense to مَن or ما, which may in themselves connote either a defined or an undefined entity [§4 : 7]: هو مِمَّن عرفته مُنْذُ صِغَرى 'he is a person whom I have known since my youth'; مِمّا يُلاحَظُ أنَّ . . . 'a thing which should be noticed is that . . .'.

§15 : 7. When the direct object of a verb is a pronoun, one may occasionally find, in lieu of prepositional substitution after the verbal abstract or participle, qualifying pronoun forms [§2 : 16] attached to حبّها إيّاىَ 'my love of her', حبّى إيّاها :إيّا 'her love of me'.

§15 : 8. Participle forms can be annexed to the direct object term, or if requisite the latter can be replaced by the prepositional substitution with لِ; these structures are normal when the participle is used as a noun. But

if it has the sense of an adjective, the direct object term can retain the
نصب form it would have after the verb:

كل مُخالِفِـى سياستِنَا   'all the opponents of our policy'

هم مخالفون لطَرَفٍ من سياسِتِنا   'they are opponents of one aspect
of our policy'

هم مخالفون طرفًا من سياستنا   'they are opposing one aspect of
our policy'

§15 : 9. The نصب for the direct object can also be retained after a
verbal abstract: اعتناق المسلمين النصرانية ‎ 'the Muslims' embracing of
Christianity'.

16

QUERIES, COMMANDS AND EXCLAMATIONS

§16 : 1. When a proposition is queried instead of stated, أ or هَلْ is placed in front of the normal statement structure: هل يذهب الامير 'is the prince going?'; أفى هذا صعوبة 'is there any difficulty in this?'. It is a special peculiarity of أ that it is placed in front of the basic connectives: أفتعتقدون هذا 'do you then believe this?'.

§16 : 2. If the query is posed in the form of two alternatives, أمْ is placed in front of the second alternative: أيذهب الامير أم الوزير 'is it the prince or the minister who is going?'; أعلمت هذا أم لا 'did you know this or not?' [§9 : 13].

§16 : 3. مَنْ 'who?' and ما or ماذا 'what?' can either be treated as themes having a subsequent pronoun referring back to them, or as sentence elements displaced from their normal position to the beginning of the sentence. In this displacement they are accompanied by any preposition belonging to them:

$$\left.\begin{array}{l} \text{من هو فى البيت} \\ \text{من فى البيت} \end{array}\right\} \text{ 'who is in the house?'}$$

$$\left.\begin{array}{l} \text{من تقول له هذا} \\ \text{لمن تقول هذا} \end{array}\right\} \text{ 'to whom do you say this?'}$$

The ما which asks a question, when it is preceded by a preposition, is shortened to مَ and often written as one word with the preposition: علامَ يعتمد 'on what does he rely?', مِمَّ ينتج هذا 'from what does this result?' [§4 : 10]. Observe that لِمَ 'for what?/why?' will have to be distinguished from the negative لَمْ [§9 : 4].

§16 : 4. أَيّ, أَيَّة 'which?' can also function in either of the two structures referred to above:

أَيّ الكتب ترغب فيه
فى أَيّ الكتب ترغب
'which of the books do you desire?'

§16 : 5. Queries in any of the above structures can function as entity-terms serving as object of a verb: سألناه من يذهب 'we asked him who would go', نشكّ فى أيّهم جاهل بهذا 'we are doubtful about which of them is ignorant of this'. In this type of structure, أ and هل must be rendered by 'whether': قد سألناه هل يذهبون 'we have asked him whether they will go'. But in modern style, it is common in this structure to replace أ or هل by إذا or إذا ما in فى with the following clause in the structure of a conditioning one [§12 : 1] (an idiom comparable with English use of 'if' in such cases): نشكّ فى ما إذا كانت فى هذا صعوبة 'we are doubtful whether there is any difficulty in this'; سنستفهم إذا كان فى نيّته أن يذهب 'we will enquire if it is in his mind to go'.

§16 : 6. Commands are expressed by verb forms evolved by removing the first syllable from the جزم of the imperfect; if this process results in a word pattern with initial unvowelled consonant, it will be necessary to prefix *alif* [§S : 22]: فكّروا فى هذا 'think about this!'; اتركوه 'leave it alone!' (both addressed to several persons); إبْقَ 'stay!'; تَعَال (Type VI from ع . ل . و) 'come on!' (addressed to one man). Command forms of Type IV verbs, however, always begin with '*a-*, whether or not the first consonant of the root is vowelled: أَجِبْ 'answer!'. Commands expressed in this way are always positive, since the negative command, or prohibition, is expressed by the structure described in §14 : 3 (ii).

§16 : 7. There are one or two irregular command forms. e.g. سَلْ 'ask!' (root س . أ . ل), and خُذْ 'take!' (root أ . خ . ذ).

§16 : 8. When a command is followed immediately (with no connective) by a جزم imperfect, the latter expresses the anticipated result of obedience to the command: سَلْهُ يُجِبْكَ 'ask him, and he will answer you'.

§16 : 9. Exclamatory utterances tend to be idiosyncratic. One type has previously been described in §10 : 13. The نصب is also used in this function: أيّة أىّ الحَذَرَ منهم 'beware of them!'; عجيبًا 'marvellous!'. أىُّ خَطَأ أَخْطَأَه is also used exclamatorily (with or without ما inserted): 'what a mistake he made!'; انزعج لهذا الطلب أَيَّا انزعاج 'he was most terribly alarmed at this request!' [§13 : 17].

§16 : 10. When a person is addressed by name, يا is ordinarily placed before the name; when the address is by a description the descriptive noun has the article and is preceded by (يا) أَيُّها : أَيها القارىء الكريم 'gentle reader!', يا فاطمة 'Fatimah!',

17

SOME MISCELLANEOUS FUNCTIONALS

§17 : 1. ما is perhaps the most difficult word in Arabic for the beginner
to deal with, because of its enormous variety of functions. In addition
to those already mentioned [§§4 : 6, 9 : 1, 12 : 6, 16 : 3], it may be used

  (i) as a substitute for اَنْ, or for اَنْ plus perfect verb, introducing
a noun clause [§6 : 5], as in بعد أن ذهب = بعد ما ذهب 'after he went';

  (ii) after an undefined noun, reinforcing the sense of indefiniteness:
رجلٌ ما 'some man or other'.

§17 : 2. حَتَّى is used

  (i) before a نصب imperfect, to denote either (a) purpose, and thus
congruous in sense with كى [§14 : 2 (ii)], as in سألوه حتى يُوقِنوا هذا 'they
questioned him in order to ascertain this', or (b) that the following clause
describes a terminus ad quem which was not necessarily realized in fact,
as in انتظر حتى ينصرفوا 'he waited for them to depart';

  (ii) before a perfect, or a رفع imperfect, or اَنْ with a thematic
sentence structure, to denote a factual consequence or an objective which
was in fact realized, as in انتظروا حتى ذهب 'they waited until he did
depart'; قد بحثوا هذا حتى (أنهم) يعرفون حقيقته 'they have investigated
this, so that they know the truth of it'. This usage of حتى, when it
follows a negative, requires idiomatic recasting in English, as exemplified
in: لم نَنْتَهِ عن القول حتى بدأ بموضوع جديد 'before we had finished
speaking, he began on a new topic'; لم نَكَدْ ننتهى عن القول حتى بدأ
بموضوع جديد 'scarcely had we finished speaking when he began on a
new topic';

  (iii) before an entity-term (the إعراب of which is unaffected), with
the sense of 'even', as حتى الاطفال يعرفون هذا 'even children know this';

(iv) as a preposition meaning 'as far as', thus قد بحثوه حتى العَمْقِ 'they have investigated it to the very bottom'.

§17 : 3. لَمّا and إذْ (or إذ أَنْ followed by thematic sentence structure) are both used in two ways, either as a purely temporal 'when' or in the causal sense of 'because' (as with English 'since' used both temporally and causally). The differentiation between them is that the clause following لمّا depicts a situation anterior in time to that of the main statement, while the clause following إذ depicts one contemporaneous with the main statement*: لمّا أخبرهم بهذا ذهب 'when he had told them this, he went'; لما وجدنا هذا غير صحيح يمكن أنْ نُغْفِلَه 'since we have found this to be untrue, we can disregard it', كان إذ اعتزل يفكّر فى العَوْدة الى وَطَنه 'he was, when he resigned, thinking of returning to his homeland'; اذ كانت الحالة على هذا عادوا 'since the situation was thus, they returned'.

After a clause which is introduced by بَيْنَما or بَيْنا 'while', the beginning of the principal statement is normally signalized by إذ : بينا نحن فى ذلك إذ وصل رسول 'while we were engaged on that, a messenger arrived'.

§17 : 4. The use of إذا to introduce a conditioning clause [§12 : 4] or a query clause [§16 : 5] has already been mentioned. It can, however, also begin a complete sentence in thematic structure; the theme being marked either by رفع or by the preposition *bi*. The function of this structure is to add an effect of special vividness or picturesqueness to the statement: مضيت عن البيت وإذا الممثلون على الباب 'I walked out of the house, and there were the actors at the door!'; دخلنا الغُرْفة وإذا بالامير قد مات 'we entered the room, and there was the prince lying dead!'.

§17 : 5. إذا is occasionally used synonymously with لمّا, as: اذا انتهت الحرب اخذت الآمال تذوب 'when the war had ended, hopes began

---

*Though in modern usage لمّا is showing some tendency to encroach on the domain of إذ.

fading'; an ambiguity is thereby created, since this structure could formally (and in a suitable context) be interpreted as 'when the war ends, hopes will begin fading'. This usage of إذا is, however, regular in the combination فكّر فى هذه السياسة حتى إذا بَتَّ رَأْيَه فيها أخبر :حتى اذا الامير بها 'he thought about this policy until, when he had formed his opinion on it, he communicated it to the prince'.

§17 : 6. The combination of the preposition كَ with أَنَّ (or أَنْ plus perfect verbal sentence structure) has special idiomatic senses; contrary to the usual principles [§6 : 5 (i, ii)], the following proposition is not necessarily factual. The combination is commonly used to introduce a clause containing a simile: سَعَى عن الغرفة كَأَنَّه مجنون 'he ran out of the room as if he were mad'.

§17 : 7. كَأَنَّ can also be placed in front of a complete sentence in thematic structure, and then has the effect of toning down the statement if it is felt to be too bald and categorical in its unmodified form; English has various means of doing this, a common one being the insertion of 'seem' into the statement: كَأَنَّكَ تجهل بهذا 'you seem to be ignorant of this'; كَأَنَّ الحكومةَ لا تَهْتَمُّ بهذه المسألة 'the government seems to pay no attention to this problem'.

§17 : 8. إنَّما placed in front of a sentence (the structure of which it does not modify) has the effect of putting a special emphasis on the last member (clause, phrase or word) of the sentence: إنَّما اهتممنا بهذا 'it was with this in particular that we concerned ourselves'; إنَّما اهممنا بهذا لغرض 'it was for a particular reason that we concerned ourselves with this'. This emphasis is, however, often very much weakened, and may have little more than the force of English 'but', 'still', 'only': قد يكون هذا صحيحًا وإنَّما يحتاج الى برهان 'this may well be true, but it needs proof'.

§17 : 9. رُبَّ annexed to an undefined singular noun corresponds to English 'many a . . .': رب صعوبةٍ لاقيناها فى هذا 'we have encountered many a difficulty in this'. رُبَّما has the sense 'perhaps', 'probably', 'frequently', and may be inserted anywhere in the sentence structure without affecting the structure: كان ربّما أكبرَ كتّابنا 'he was perhaps the greatest of our writers'.

§17 : 10. *la-* is occasionally used (in addition to the usages mentioned §§3 : 22, 6 : 3 (i), 12 : 7) for adding emphasis: لَقَلَّ من نجا من هذا 'few indeed are those who have escaped from this'.

18

DUAL NUMBER AND NUMERALS

§18 : 1. In addition to word forms appropriate to the singular and to the plural, which in Arabic implies more than two entities, Arabic also uses a 'dual' when the reference is to two individual entities of a category. In nouns and adjectives, this is indicated by the termination ان for the رفع, or يْنِ for نصب and جرّ, added to the singular form. When the word is annexed, the final syllable of this termination is dropped. Hence, الجوابان فى معنًى واحد 'the two answers are in one single sense'; الاستنتاج من الجوابَيْنِ واضح 'the inference from the two answers is obvious; دولتا مصر والاردن مُتوافِقتانِ على هذا 'the states of Egypt and Jordan are in mutual agreement over this'; فى دولتَىْ مصر والاردن 'in the states of Egypt and Jordan'.

§18 : 2. Dual forms of pronouns show no differentiation between masculine and feminine. The following are the forms:

Singular	Dual	Singular	Dual
هو هى	هُما	أنْتَ أنْتِ	أنْتُما
ـه ـها	ـهُما	لكَ لكِ	كُما

§18 : 3. In the perfect verb, the correspondances are:

Singular	Dual	Singular	Dual
فَعَلَ	فَعَلا	فَعَلْتَ / فَعَلْتِ	فَعَلْتُما
فَعَلَتْ	فَعَلَتا		

§18 : 4. In the imperfect verb, the رفع forms are: singular يَفْعَلُ, dual يَفْعَلانِ; singular تَفْعَلُ, dual تَفْعَلانِ. In نصب and جزم these dual forms drop the final syllable.

§18 : 5. As with the plural [§3 : 17] a singular verb precedes a dual clarificatory entity-term: انصرف الرجلانِ 'the two men departed'.

§18 : 6. Dual demonstratives, unlike their singular and plural counter-parts, show differentiation between رفع on one hand, and نصب and جرّ on the other; the differentiation resembles that found in the dual termina-tions of nouns and adjectives [§18 : 1].

Singular	هذا	هذه	ذلك	تلك
Dual	هٰذان/هٰذين ِ	هٰتان/هٰتين ِ	ذانِّك/ذَيْنِّك َ	تانِّك/تَيْنِّك َ

§18 : 7. The same is the case with the dual forms of الّتى الّذى, which are الَّذان/الَّذَيْن, الّتان/التَّيْن. It should be noted that the choice of forms is dictated by the functional relationship between these forms and the main statement; the functional position of the pronoun, within the qualifying clause, which looks back to these words is irrelevant to the choice of forms:

اعتزل الوزيران الذان استشرتهما　　'the two ministers whom I con-sulted have resigned'

استشرت الوزيرين الذين اعتزلا　　'I consulted the two ministers who resigned'

§18 : 8. Because of the existence of the dual forms, the Arabic numeral 'two' is relatively rarely used. It has the form اثْنـ [§S : 23] plus the termi-nations characteristic of the masculine and feminine dual of nouns: لاَ تْنَتَيْن ِ من النساء 'for two of the women'.

§18 : 9. Duality can be emphasized by the use of an annexed entity-term meaning 'both of . . .'. When annexed to nouns, this has the invariable forms كلا (masculine) and كِلْتا (feminine): لكلتا هتين الدولتين 'for both of these states'. When annexed to pronouns, these forms vary positionally as do dual nouns: كلاهما جاهلان على السَّواء 'both of them are equally ignorant'; كلّمت كلتَيْهما 'I spoke to both of them (females)'.

This traditional form, while still in use, is nevertheless tending in modern style to be replaced by فى كلتا هاتين الدولتين : كلٌّ من = فى كلٌّ من هاتين الدولتين 'in both these two states'.

§18 : 10. The numeral 'one' is also relatively rarely used, in view of the structures described §§1 : 3, 1 : 17. See also §1 : 18 on the noun إحدى/أحد.

The form واحدة, واحد can be used as adjective or noun, either of persons or things.

§18 : 11. بَعْض annexed to a dual pronoun signifies in modern usage 'each other': جلسا إلى جانب بعضهما 'the two of them sat beside each other'. In traditional Arabic this is expressed by the structure جلس بعضُهما الى جانب بعضٍ ('one of them sat beside one'), and this traditional structure will still be encountered in modern writing.

§18 : 12. The numerals 3 to 10 are annexed to the noun numbered, which is plural. The numeral forms terminate in ة when the entity numbered is masculine in the singular, but without ة when it is feminine in the singular: أَرْبَعة رجال 'four men'; أَرْبَع ممثلات 'four actresses'.

§18 : 13. After numerals from 11 to 99 the noun numbered is in the نصب of the singular; those from 100 upwards are annexed to the singular noun.

§18 : 14. In the numerals 13 to 19, the unit element behaves according to the principle stated in §18 : 13, but the 'ten' in the reverse way. All the forms are devoid of إعراب and are uniformly vocalized with terminal -a: خَمْسَ عَشْرَةَ رجلاً 'fifteen men'; خَمْسة عَشَرَ ممثلةً 'fifteen actresses'.

§18 : 15. The numeral 11 is also devoid of إعراب, its ten element behaving as with 13 to 19, the 'one' element agreeing in form with the noun: أَحَدَ عَشَرَ رجلاً 'eleven men', إحْدَى عَشْرَةَ ممثلةً 'eleven actresses'. In the numeral 12, the 'two' element has the terminal variations of a dual [§18 : 1]: جاءَ اثْنا عَشَرَ رجلاً 'twelve men came'; لقيتُ اثْنَىْ عَشَرَ رجلاً 'I met twelve men'; رأيتُ اثْنَتَىْ عَشْرَةَ ممثلةً 'I saw twelve actresses'; جاءت اثْنَتا عَشْرَةَ ممثلةً 'twelve actresses came'.

§18 : 16. The numerals 20, 30, etc., up to 90 have no differentiation between masculine and feminine, but have terminations resembling those of the masculine plural described in §13 : 17: حضر عِشْرونَ رجلاً 'twenty men were present'; كلّم خَمْسِينَ ممثلةً 'he spoke to fifty actresses'.

§18 : 17. مائة 'a hundred' [§§S : 27 (i)] is devoid of differentiation between masculine and feminine, and retains the singular form when preceded by unit numerals, but has a dual and a plural in other circumstances: أربعمئة رجلٍ 'four hundred men' [§13 : 8], حضر مائتا رجلٍ 'two hundred men were present'; قتلوا مائتى رجلٍ 'they killed two hundred men'; مئات من الأطنان 'hundreds of tons'. ألْف 'a thousand' behaves in every way like a noun except in the form exhibited by the numbered entity: سبعة آلاف رجلٍ 'seven thousand men'.

§18 : 18. The annexion structure whereby 'one' in annexion is not made defined [§1 : 7] is in contemporary Arabic sometimes extended to other numerals: أخذ ألُوف الأسْرَى 'thousands of prisoners were taken'.

§18 : 19. The word pattern فاعـل is used to construct ordinal numerals from 2 to 10: ثان [§13 : 12] 'second', رابـِع 'fourth', etc.; although سادِس 'sixth' is anomalous in relation to the numeral 'six'. For the larger numbers, there are no distinctive forms, and the basic numeral forms are employed also as ordinals: الباب المائة 'the hundredth chapter'.

APPENDIX

Abbreviations are relatively little used in Arabic, but the reader may well encounter the following:

(1) الخ (occasionally (اه) = الى آخِرِه and stands for 'etc.'.

(2) The word الآية is commonly employed for 'etc.' in quotations from the Qur'ān.

(3) In dates, the Christian era is denoted by م (= مِيْلَادِى), the Muslim era by هِ (= هِجْرِى). ق.م. (= قبل الميلاد) 'B.C.'.

(4) ج = مُجَلَّد 'volume', ص = صَفْحة 'page', and س = سَطْر 'line'.

ADDENDA

p. 44, §3 : 11 at end
Verbal abstracts of Types IV, VII, VIII and X (together with other noun patterns which have $\bar{a}$ before the third consonant of the root), when formed from roots ending in *w* or *y*, show a change of the *w* or *y* to *hamʒa* (cp. §8 : 8).

p. 91, §13 : 11 line 10 of the para., read
hamʒa preceded by $\bar{a}$ or *a*.

114

ENGLISH INDEX

In the case of references marked with an asterisk, the reader should also consult the 'Addenda'.